Acquired Self

The Basis Of All Sufferings

LEARN HOW TO BE FREE OF IT

Sarfraz Zaidi, MD

Acquired Self - The Basis Of All Sufferings

Learn How To Be Free Of It

ISBN: 978-0-9887844-7-5

icomet press

Camarillo, CA.

USA

Email: contact@doctorzaidi.com

DISCLAIMER

The information in this book is true and complete to the best of our knowledge. What you are about to read are author's own independent observations. Let it be very clear that the author does not belong to any organization: political, religious, non-religious, cultural etc. Author has no hidden agenda. Author is not on any mission either. Author is simply sharing his independent observations with you.

This book is intended only as an informative guide for those wishing to know more about health issues. The information in this book is not intended to replace the advice of a health care provider. The author and publisher disclaim any liability for the decisions you make based on the information contained in this book. The information provided herein should not be used during any medical emergency or for the diagnosis and treatment of any medical condition. In no way is this book intended to replace, countermand or conflict with the advice given to you by your own health care provider. The information contained in this book is general and is offered with no guarantees on the part of the author or publisher. The author and publisher disclaim all liability in connection with the use of this book. Any duplication or distribution of information contained herein is strictly prohibited.

This book is intended for those

who use common sense and stay open-minded.

TABLE OF CONTENTS

INTRODUCTION

Believe it or not, most of the world is in a deep psychological sleep, busy with their mundane life – full of stress, diseases, conflicts – and have no clue what is really happening.

So was I, living a so-called successful life, filled with achievements, money, excitement, and praise but there was no inner peace, no contentment, no real joy. Slowly, I started to wake up from the toxic sleep of greed, ego, fear, anger, and jealousy, to name a few demons.

One day, as I was walking in my neighborhood park, pondering over the root cause of stress and human suffering, I was struck by Divine Wisdom. which would change my life forever. In that moment, I shrugged off my false identity, which I call the Acquired Self.

Once the fog of the Acquired Self cleared up, I was in touch with my True Self, automatically without practicing any techniques. Instantaneously, my heart was filled with unconditional love, peace, and joy. I started jumping in the park with ecstasy.

Since that day in the park, I have stayed free of stress and its horrendous consequences. I keep my awareness in the NOW, most of the time.

As an awakened soul, I opted not to renunciate the world, *although it was tempting*. Instead, I embraced the world, and my innate empathy would put me on a path to awaken my fellow human beings.

First, I incorporated Divine Wisdom in my medical practice and shifted my focus to *curing* diseases instead of just managing them through medications. The results were gratifying.

I also share this Divine Wisdom with fellow human beings wherever I encounter them, in parks, beaches, coffee shops, restaurants, gyms, saunas, pickleball clubs, and hiking groups. In addition, I share this Divine Wisdom with the world through articles, videos, and books. However, let me be very clear that I am *not* on any mission. I am simply guiding people to live a life that is filled with inner peace, joy, and unconditional love.

Welcome aboard! Read this book slowly, using common sense and an open mind. Put this Divine Wisdom into practice and see the results for yourself.

Sincerely,

Sarfraz Zaidi, MD

CHAPTER: 1

YOU ARE NOT WHO YOU THINK YOU ARE

If I were to ask, "Who do you think you are?" You may reply, "I am Lisa, a physician, a Canadian, a liberal, a Catholic etc."

Really?

If I were to meet you without knowing anything about you, I wouldn't know that you are Lisa, a physician, a Canadian, a liberal, a Catholic, right? Instead, I will see you as a human being, no more, no less.

Unfortunately, everyone thinks they are their name, profession, nationality, religion, etc.

Let us use common sense and explore who you really are. At birth you were REAL, right? A live human being, but you did not have a name, profession, nationality, religion, etc. You acquired these labels as you grew up in society, right? These labels are basically concepts, no more.

Imagine if you were not raised in a human society, but in Nature. Then, you would not have a name, profession, nationality, religion, etc. In fact, you would not even be thinking in a human language such as English, German, Hindi, etc. because people acquire human languages as they grow up in a human society.

At birth you are alive human beings. You are equipped with innate intelligence, but you do not think in a human language. Thinking comes later as you grow up in human society and learn the human language of that society. Hence, we can conclude that you are not who you think you are.

Whatever you think of yourself consists of the concepts that you acquire as you grow up in society. We can call it your Acquired Self, as you acquired it from society, but you were not born with this. In contrast, you are born with a Self that we can call the original, True Self, which is devoid of any concepts – no name, profession, nationality, religion, etc.

With few exceptions, everyone is in the grip of their Acquired Self. That's who they think they are.

The Acquired Self is the root cause of all suffering, as I discuss later in this book. From emotional stress to physical diseases to conflicts and wars, the Acquired Self lies at the root. Even global warming and Artificial Intelligence (AI) are due to the Acquired Self.

CHAPTER: 2

MY OWN AWAKENING

Is it possible to live a stress-free life in this stressed-out world?

I asked this question myself, as I was living a very stressful life. On the surface, I was successful, accomplished, and loved by my family and friends but something was missing. There was no inner peace. I had moments of thrills and excitement, but inner joy was lacking. I would keep chasing one goal after another. There was no contentment.

At the age of forty-seven, I started having anxiety attacks. I did not want to go on anti-anxiety medications. Instead, I wanted to cure my anxiety disorder naturally. This was the turning point for me. I had to find an answer. That's how my journey to awakening started.

After reading a few books on stress management, it became clear that the root of our stress is the "Self." "But if I am not my "Self," then who am I?" was my question.

The Park Incidence

One day as I was walking in our neighborhood park, I asked, “Who am I?” There was no answer. Then, I decided to use an alternative approach that we physicians use to diagnose tough cases: the process of ruling out. We rule out various causes one by one, until we get to the correct diagnosis. To find out who I really am, I decided to see who I am NOT.

Using logic, I realized that I was still myself before I became a specialist, bought a home, and owned a luxury car. I was still myself before I became a husband. I was still myself before I went to medical school, college, and high school. I was still myself before I started elementary school. I was still myself before I started talking, walking, standing, crawling, and sitting. I was still myself when I was born… So, I was myself - the REAL me - when I was born and everything else, I acquired later in life from society, which I called the Acquired Self.

In reality, I am not the Acquired Self. Therefore, I am not Sarfraz Zaidi, in real. It is Sarfraz Zaidi that has been carrying all the emotional burden of the past and worries about future.

With this realization, a shocking sensation went through my body. Then there was relief, as if a huge load was lifted off my shoulders. Then, there was a feeling of inner peace, freedom, and joy.

Book Starts Writing Itself

I came home and told my wife what had happened. She said, "you have lost your mind, go to sleep," but I could not go to sleep. I was having a flood of *new* thoughts that I did not know before. My wife is an accomplished writer. She advised me to start writing, which I did. By 3 am, I had written 70 pages.

The Day After

The next morning, I wondered how I was when I was born. Of course, I did not know how I was at birth. Fortunately, I had the opportunity to oversee a well-baby nursery in my early career and observed about sixty newborn babies every day. Later, I had the wonderful experience of having my own baby. I reflected on those experiences. What I realized would change my life forever.

You, me and everyone else on the planet are born with a self that we can call the True Self, which I will discuss in detail in the next chapter.

The Challenge Of A Physical Illness

A few months after the Park Incidence, I developed an illness (Ulcerative Colitis) which has no cure. Symptoms can be managed by use of immunosuppressive drugs, but I wanted to cure it. I saw several brilliant doctors, but everyone gave the same answer: no cure.

I am fortunate that the illness happened after I had gotten Divine Wisdom. The previous me would have been miserable, but I walked on this road without any stress. I would simply stay in the NOW and would not experience any emotional stress. Even the physical stress from the illness did not bother me, although my loved ones were getting quite stressed out, because I had lost a significant amount of weight. One day, my wife accurately pointed out, "you look like someone from a concentration camp," as she saw me in the shower.

I realized that even the act of talking would exhaust me. I spent more time in my bedroom and in the backyard. In this way, I kept myself in the NOW. More wisdom kept sinking in. At one point, I became free of the fear of death.

Ultimately, I was able to cure this seemingly incurable illness.

Divine Is REAL

One day, I was having lunch at a restaurant by myself. It was a windy day. I was looking at the branches of some big, old trees that were swinging wildly. I was completely in the NOW, paying attention to stillness while watching the movement of the branches. There were no thoughts whatsoever. Suddenly, I was in a different dimension: a dimension of profound stillness, silence, and space, although words don't quite describe it. I was awake, aware of other people in the restaurant, but it was as if they were in the background. In the foreground was this immense stillness, silence, and space. It was utterly powerful, but very peaceful. No words can accurately describe it. Then an inner voice popped, “This is God.”

Then the waiter came and asked me something, which got me out of this dimension, but immense peace was still there in my chest.

Please be advised, I am using the word God simply to communicate with you. The word itself is not Real God, who also has no description.

Since that day in the restaurant, I can get into this dimension by sitting quietly by myself and keeping my attention completely in the NOW, without any thinking. In this state, I also get original thoughts. I call it Divine Wisdom, which I am sharing with you in this book.

Holistic Healing Starts

I implemented newly found wisdom into my medical practice and took the following steps:

I switched from being a doctor who relied on prescribing medications to a more comprehensive, holistic healer. I realized that stress lies at the root of all diseases. Therefore, I needed time to explain my wisdom on how to be stress-free. Hence, I cut down my schedule from 25 patients a day to only 10, so I could spend enough time with each patient.

In addition, I started to question all the concepts of modern medicine. For example, I started clinical research to find out if people living in sunny places like southern California had adequate levels of Vitamin D, as Vitamin D plays a crucial role in keeping us healthy. To my utter surprise, every patient (except one) turned out to be low in Vitamin D, despite taking a Vitamin D supplement 400 IU per day, being in the sun for more than 15 minutes a day and eating fish three times a week. According to prevailing medical knowledge, all these patients should have adequate levels of Vitamin D. However, the facts pointed in the opposite direction.

I realized that I was trained to be a prescriber, not a healer. I decided to be a healer from here onwards. Therefore, I started to explore vitamins and herbs that could heal my patients. In addition, I took a dive into meditation, yoga, nutrition, exercise, rest, and sleep. Finally, I came up with a comprehensive, holistic approach to health, called SNEVM, which is an acronym.

SNEVM

S: Stress cure

N: Nutrition

E: Exercise, rest, sleep

V: Vitamins, herbs

M: Medications only when necessary

I started seeing amazing outcomes in my patients. For example, patients with high blood pressure were able to reduce or even completely stop their blood pressure medications. Type 2 diabetic patients were able to come off insulin and other anti-diabetic drugs. Patients with thyroid diseases were curing Hashimoto's thyroiditis and Graves' disease. Most of my elderly patients did not have any heart attacks, strokes or dementia. No one broke their hips or spine due to osteoporosis.

The single most important factor for these great results was my wisdom on how to live a stress-free life, that I will share with you in this book.

CHAPTER: 3

THE TRUE SELF

Do you remember a time in your life when you did not have any emotional stress whatsoever? Most people would reply, "No."

You may be surprised to know that everyone is totally stress-free (emotionally speaking) when they start out their journey in this life span. Why? Because they are grounded in their True Self.

To know your "True, REAL Self, " observe little babies, just a day or so old.

Joyful And Peaceful

When I observe little babies, I see they are joyful and peaceful from within, as soon as their basic needs are met: a full stomach, a clean diaper, a warm blanket, a loving human being, such as a mother or father.

No Past Or Future

Babies have no past or future. They don't think about what has already happened or what may happen. They are not worried if mom will be around for the next feed. If they did, they wouldn't be able to go to sleep.

Living In The Now

Babies are joyful just looking around. They truly live in the Now. They do it spontaneously without learning any techniques on how to live in the Now.

Playful And Joyful

Babies are so playful and joyful just by interacting with whatever is in their field of awareness such as people, animals, flowers, trees, breeze, sky, etc.

Curious

Babies are curious about whatever they experience through their senses. For example, they are curious about the bird, the cat, and the dog that they see. They are curious about the sounds they hear, the food they taste, and fragrances they smell. By using their senses, they also learn what is pleasurable, what is painful, what is soothing, what is irritating, what is warm, and what is cold, etc.

Contented

Once their stomach is full, babies don't want any more food. If you were to force more food than they need, they would regurgitate. They eat to satisfy their hunger and that's all. "Wanting more" does not exist and that's why they are so content.

Practical

Babies are also very practical. You could feed them breast milk, cow's milk or formula. To them, it doesn't matter as long as food agrees with their stomach and satisfies their hunger.

No Fear

Babies are so vulnerable, but fear remains miles away. There is a total lack of control, but no fear whatsoever.

No Religion or Nationality

No baby comes in this world and announces that she is a Christian, Muslim, Hindu, etc. They don't say "I am a Canadian, Indian, German, Russian, etc.

No Likes or Dislikes

Babies don't say "I don't like your milk, Mom. I like formula milk better." You won't hear, "Mom, you wrapped me in a pink blanket with butterflies on it. I'm a boy. Therefore, I need a blue blanket with pictures of dinosaurs."

No Judging or Interpretation

Newborn babies don't like or dislike someone because of their color, religion, nationality, or wealth. That's because they have not acquired any concepts about religion, nationality, history, or money.

Concepts do not exist at all. Likes and dislikes do not exist. There are no preferences or judgments. No embarrassment or shame being nude.

No Thinking

Babies don't think the way we adults think. Why do I say newborn babies don't think? Because we always think in terms of the language we have learned. For example, if you know English and no other language, you will always think in English, not in Chinese, French, or Hindi. Just observe it right now. You are reading (and thinking) in English, a language you have learned.

To think, we need to know a language. Therefore, language is the basis of thinking.

Newborns do not know any language. Hence, they don't think. It is so logical, isn't it? They also don't have any concepts. Why? Because concepts arise out of language. No language - no concepts.

Universal Divine Intelligence

We assume a person to be unintelligent if they can't think. So, if newborn babies don't think, are they unintelligent? Not at all. Quite the opposite. Put a newborn baby on their mom's chest. In no time, the baby will find a nipple and start to suckle their food. Pretty intelligent!

They will let you know if they are hungry, cold or wet. Caring parents can figure out their baby's needs from the type of cry - whether it is time to feed, change the diaper, or carry the baby in their loving arms. This is how babies communicate clearly with their parents.

Babies look at their parents – soul to soul – which leads to inseparable bonding. When a mother breast-feeds her baby, another bonding takes place through the release of a hormone, Oxytocin, in the mother's brain. Perhaps there are many other mechanisms we don't know about because of the limitations of our thinking mind.

Babies live in the Now. In this way, they stay in touch with the "Fabric of the Universe" that we "grown-ups" have not been able to figure out using the filters of our thinking mind.

Babies don't think and that's why their attention remains in the reality of the Now. In this way, they stay connected with Universal Intelligence.

In summary*, you, me and everyone else on the planet are born with a Self that is our True Self. It naturally lives in the Now, without any effort. It is free of the long shadows of the past or clouds of the future. It has no fear, no anger, no hate, no wanting more, no prejudices, no shame, no guilt, no disappointments, no grievances, no religions, no nationalities, no races, no history... Just pure joy, contentment, peace, curiosity, and playfulness. It interacts with everyone and everything that is in its field of awareness. It stays connected with the Divine (as it is a manifestation of the Divine), and everyone else by using Universal Divine Intelligence.*

CHAPTER: 4

THE ACQUIRED SELF

Now let's see what happens to this fearless, non-judging, contented, peaceful, and joyful human being.

The Baby grows up in society and that changes everything drastically. Every society downloads a never-ending list of concepts into the mind of the growing baby. At the core of the layers of the concepts is the concept of "I," which steals our identity. We can call it the Acquired Self, because we acquire it from society.

As we grow up, this Acquired Self continues to get bigger. Gradually it gets in the driver's seat, pushing the True Self onto the passenger side, then the back seat, and eventually into the trunk. Just an analogy!

As grown-ups, all we see is this Acquired Self. We totally identify with it. That's who we think we are. In this way, our identity gets hijacked by the Acquired Self. Instead of seeing the hijacker for what it is, we think that's who we are. How ironic!

This Acquired Self is the basis of all our emotional stress. It reacts to outside triggers, which it calls stressors and blames them for its stress. In fact, it is the Acquired Self that reacts to triggers and creates stress for us. In this way, the source of all stress really resides inside us, and not out there. It is good to know this basic fact. Why? Because if the source of stress is inside us, so is the solution.

This Acquired Self torments us and creates stress even when there is no stressful situation. It conveniently creates hypothetical situations (the What If Syndrome) to make us fearful.

Therefore, we can call Acquired Self the enemy within. Unfortunately, we get out of touch with our True Self, the source of true joy, contentment, and inner peace. In the total grip of the Acquired Self, we suffer and suffer. We create stress not only for ourselves, but for others as well.

Q: *Tell me how can I find my True Self?*

A: All you have to do is free yourself from the Acquired Self, the curtain that hides your True Self. Think of your True Self as the Sun and the Acquired Self as the clouds. The Sun is always shining, though it may be blocked by the clouds. The denser the clouds, the less visible the Sun. However, the Sun is visible as soon as the clouds disappear.

CHAPTER: 5

MAKING OF THE ACQUIRED SELF

The Acquired Self is a product of society, which itself is a Collective Acquired Self. (More on it later in the book)

We could call our personal Acquired Self the "baby monster" and the Collective Acquired Self of society the "papa monster." Just an analogy.

I use the word monster just for the sake of description without any negativity attached to it.

The papa monster downloads itself into the baby monster and continues to feed it for the rest of its life. As the baby monster grows up, it feeds itself back to the papa monster. In this way, the two are intertwined and continue to feed each other.

The main purpose of our Acquired Self is for us to be able to function in society, but problems arises when it steals our identity - we start to believe it is who we are. Then it becomes a source of never-ending stress.

There are <u>three</u> mechanisms which create our personal Acquired Self:

- Psychosocial conditioning.
- Instillation of information.
- Creation of past and future.

Let's take a closer look at each of these mechanisms.

CHAPTER: 6

PSYCHOSOCIAL CONDITIONING

Psychosocial conditioning plays a major part in creating our Acquired Self. It starts at home. Parents and grandparents play their role in conditioning our mind. Then, school comes, where teachers sincerely do their share to condition our mind. Later, it's society in general that continues to condition our mind.

Concept Of "I"

At birth, our parents put a carefully selected label on us. They call it our Name, which is basically a sound. Our parents utter this sound as they point towards us. After doing it repeatedly, they finally succeed in drilling into our head that we are indeed Peter, Lisa, or Ali, etc. This is the birth of the "virtual I."

Attachments

We start getting attached to our parents who provide us with food, comfort and warmth. It works for a few months, but then our parents want some time for themselves, too. So, they look for some distractions for us. They find their answer in "toys." Initially, we are curious about these things that look cute and make funny noises. Slowly, we get attached to them. "They are mine." The concept of possessions is born.

Judging, Reward And Punishment

Now, our parents go one step further. They start to control our behavior through these toys: If we do what they tell us (good behavior), we get more toys, but if we don't do what they tell us (bad behavior), then we won't get any toys. Sometimes, they even take away our toys to punish us for not listening to them. The concepts of good behavior and bad behavior, reward and punishment are added to our growing Acquired Self.

Ego And Love

The concept of toys soon gets glorified into the concept of gifts. Now we receive toys wrapped up in paper and these are called gifts. The concept of gifts is further refined: we receive a gift because we are special and the person who gives us a gift loves us. The concepts of "I am special" and "love through gifts" are added to our growing Acquired Self.

Excitement And Boredom

"Toys, gifts, being special, and being loved" provide us momentary thrill and excitement. However, that soon fades away, and we get bored. Then, we want more momentary thrills and excitement. That's why we cannot wait until our birthday to receive more gifts.

The concept of gifts is so exciting that we cannot wait to count the gifts and open them. That is where we get most of our excitement. We may not even be interested in what is inside the package. With time, we develop an insatiable appetite for momentary thrills and excitement.

There are a lot of other ways in which our parents provide us with momentary thrills and excitement. Smart phones and video games are popular these days. Starting at a young age, we get our fixes of momentary excitement watching these virtual games. Manufacturers of these games fool our parents with sale pitches. "These are great educational tools." "This will improve your kid's dexterity." "After using our game, your child will be more advanced than the other kids in preschool."

More Judging, Reward, And Punishment

Most of these games are built around the concepts of "winning, rewards, good, and bad." We must achieve certain points, usually by killing some object (troll, demon, spy, etc.) called evil or bad. If we win, we are the good hero and a reward follows. The concepts of "bad, evil, hero, killing, winning, and losing" are added to our growing Acquired Self.

At the same time, we also start getting exposed to stories, books, movies, and plays, most of which further deepen the concepts of "good, bad, villain, hero, reward, and punishment."

We get so attached to these concepts that we love to wear T-shirts with pictures of these heroic characters (which cost our parents a whole lot more than a regular shirt!)

We also hear our parents constantly calling some events and behaviors "good" and others "bad." They also often use phrases such as "I like it," "I don't like it," "I love it," "I hate it." Soon we start to replicate these phrases.

Judging provokes intense emotions inside us in the form of thrill, excitement, sadness, horror, and fear. We may even have nightmares with random distorted replays of these mental images during our sleep.

ADHD

(Attention Deficit/Hyperactivity Disorder)

In some children, this sensory load of virtual information from video games, books and movies is so enormous that their developing brain cannot handle it. These children start to exhibit signs of sensory overload in the form of jitteriness, disruptive and impulsive behavior, and difficulty focusing. They become a problem for their teacher, who calls in the parents to have a joint meeting with a counselor at the school.

Upon the teacher's insistence, parents often take their child to a pediatrician who conveniently gives a diagnosis of ADHD (Attention Deficit/Hyperactivity Disorder). The "poor child" is then put on a drug to alter their brain chemistry. It is a band-aid approach to calm the kid down, so the classroom is not disrupted. Meanwhile, the root cause for the problem, the Acquired Self, keeps getting bigger.

Abandonment

Our parents – who are so loving and who we are so attached to – one day decides to leave us with a stranger called a baby-sitter. We feel intense emotional pain of abandonment. We cry and cry and cry! Finally, we are distracted by toys or get exhausted from crying and eventually go to sleep.

Later, when our guilt-stricken parents ask the baby-sitter how things went, she may lie. “There was no problem. Your baby is an angel, and I would love to baby-sit her again,” she says as she receives her hourly wages.

Repeated episodes of this emotionally traumatic experience of abandonment keep adding to our Acquired Self.

Note: Please be aware it’s not our parents’ fault. They are doing what society’s collective Acquired Self has advised them to do. “You should have some private quality time, just the two of you, away from your children to keep your marriage alive.”

Comparison And Judging

At home, we are compared to our brother, sister, or cousin. We may remember our dad / mom saying, “Why can’t you be like your older brother?” Comments like this trigger emotions of humiliation, worthlessness, and jealousy. All these negative comments with their associated negative emotions get added to our Acquired Self.

We also hear our parents comparing and judging people, events, and objects all the time: “Better than,” “the Best,” “Worse than,” “the Worst.”

All the comparing and judging keeps adding to our Acquired Self. Soon, we start to copy our parents. “My best friend,” “My favorite toy,” “My favorite uncle,” “My dad is the best in the whole wide world." Our parents keep reinforcing these ideas in our Acquired Self.

Rules And Consequences

At some point, we enter school. Now, the making of our Acquired Self gets into high gear. Soon we learn we cannot be at ease in the morning. Now we need to be at school on time or there will be consequences in the form of punishment. We must follow certain rules in the classroom or there will be consequences.

We also hear a lot of rules at home. Follow them or face the consequences. Initially, we resent these rules and their consequences.

We may develop resentment against those (parents and teachers) who implement these punishments. Ultimately, we may develop rebellion against authority, but we may also develop fear of authority as we know they possess the power to punish us.

At school as well as at home, we also learn the concept of how to be good and receive rewards in the form of praise, recognition, and even some money. Our parents may start rewarding us with money as an allowance for our good behavior. These rewards give us momentary excitement.

The concepts of "punishment" and "reward" keep getting deeper into our growing Acquired Self.

More Comparison And Competition

At school, comparison and competition are the main driving forces. Spelling bee competitions, captain of the football team, and student of the month are just a few examples. Kids are also enrolled in dance, gymnastics, skating, music, and speech competitions. Plus, there are all the sports competitions - Little League, soccer, basketball, track, volleyball, and football. Then there are local beauty pageants and academic decathlons. You get the idea!

Among teenagers, competition for a boyfriend or girlfriend starts to take place. Girls compare each other's looks and clothes, while boys compete in the sports arena. Often there are verbal as well as physical fights. Everyone wants to be popular, wants to be praised and acknowledged.

School often becomes a battlefield. Everyone wants to win and defeat others. The concepts of "victory" and "defeat" get embedded into our Acquired Self. Everyone wants to be a "winner" and not a "loser." However, in life we sometimes win and sometimes lose. It's a fact of life.

Each time we win, we are thrilled and feel superior to others. We receive praise and validation from those around us. We feel we are at the top of the world. It boosts our ego.

But these feelings are short-lived. Obviously, we want more of these exciting feelings.

"Wanting More" is the basis of greed and it kills all contentment. We develop chronic restlessness, constantly looking for more thrills and excitement. When we don't get our fix, we get frustrated, agitated, and bored.

On the other hand, each time we lose, we feel humiliated, inferior, worthless, and jealous; If we feel that we lost because of unfairness, then we also become bitter, resentful, hateful, revengeful, and angry.

All these emotional experiences continue to add to our Acquired Self in the form of memories - good as well as bad memories. Over the years, we accumulate tons of emotions associated with these memories, which adds to our emotional baggage.

More Judging

We continue to be judged constantly at home as well as school, in the form of our report card, good behavior, bad behavior, good attitude, bad attitude, good manners, bad manners, polite, and rude. Each time we are judged – good or bad – we feel the corresponding good or bad emotion.

Ethics and Morality

At some point, our Acquired Self is downloaded with the concept of "ethics and morality:" how everyone should and should not behave.

For example, it tells us "This is how a true friend should and should not behave… This is how a good boyfriend/girlfriend/ husband/wife should and should not behave… This is how a good parent should and should not behave… This is how a good child/student should and should not behave."

Equipped with this "concept of role description," our Acquired Self constantly judges others as good or bad, while they judge us. Each time we are judged good or bad, we feel the corresponding emotion.

Expectations

We also build up expectations around this "concept of role description," naively thinking "If I do everything by the book, then the other person will keep up his end of the deal." However, when the other person doesn't behave as expected, we get disappointed, frustrated, and sometimes outraged. The stronger the expectation, the deeper the disappointment, frustration and anger.

Self - Criticism

In addition, we also judge ourselves. When we do not (or cannot) behave according to the "concept of role description," we criticize ourselves. This is the basis of self-criticism and guilt.

I, Me, My, Mine

The concept of "I, Me, My, Mine" continues to embed deeper into our growing Acquired Self.

A few examples: "My friends," "My school," "My teacher," "My books," "My home," "My neighborhood." "Why me?" "Why not me?" "This is mine."

The Acquired Self Steals Our Identity

The concept of "I, Me, My, Mine" creates an illusion of who we are. In this way, the Acquired Self hijacks our identity. We lose our identity and start to believe in this illusory "I" to be who we are.

The innocent, joyful, contented us is hijacked by this agitated monstrous Acquired Self who wants to win at all costs. This monster always wants more (greedy), is self-centered, and carries a huge load of worthlessness, bitterness, jealousy, hate, and anger. It wants to defeat, control and humiliate others. It wants to take revenge for its previous humiliating experiences. It is always looking for momentary thrills and excitement. It is constantly judging others while others are judging it. Often it is judging itself. It looks for rewards, praise and validation. It is afraid of punishment and consequences such as disciplinary actions, bad grades, unable to secure a high school diploma or an admission into a college. It is also afraid of losing its friends, looks and health. It easily gets hurt, frustrated, and disappointed. It dwells in its past and worries about its future.

Welcome To The "Real World"

Now this monstrous, virtual "I" enters the so-called, real world, (which is not real but virtual, conceptual). Competition, comparison, and judging get even worse. We see everyone competing for money. Naturally, money becomes our main goal. We do it in the name of career and profession. We fight for jobs. Sometimes we win and sometimes we lose.

At the workplace, everyone competes for a promotion. Even when we are at the top, we want more such as more bonuses, more recognition, and more fame.

Everyone also remains scared of losing their job, promotion, and reputation.

True friendship is rare because competition and jealousy kill friendship. We compare ourselves to others all the time, just as they compare themselves to us.

Society rigorously continues to condition us through competition and comparison with the help of social media, news, and entertainment. Just see for yourself how often we hear the words "winner," "loser," "better than," "the best," "worse than," "the worst." *Every word triggers a corresponding emotion.*

Our Acquired Self becomes so competitive that even in social discussions it wants to win the argument. People don't even completely listen to each other. While one Acquired Self is making its point, the other is preparing to attack, and this goes on back and forth. Two Acquired Selves take mental positions, and no one can afford to lose the argument.

Everything in life gets focused on winning; and life becomes a battlefield. You see it everywhere: on the freeway, at work, on social media, and on TV shows. Everyone wants to get ahead. No one wants to lose.

A lot of men get hooked on watching sports. By clinging to a team, they are in a virtual competition. When our team wins, we get a momentary thrill and when it loses, we feel humiliated and even angry. This cycle continues. We get addicted to it.

Others get addicted to the win-lose cycle of sports, gambling, horse racing, car racing, board games, video games, etc. Sometimes, "emotional pains" and "desire to have momentary thrills" are so intense that a person gets addicted to alcohol, drugs or sex.

Many people also get involved in political, social and religious groups and get trapped in the cycle of "win and lose." They experience all the emotions resulting from this game of "win-lose."

All these emotional experiences keep adding to the growing monstrous Acquired Self.

While competition is usually the main driving force in the making of men's Acquired Selves, comparison becomes the driving force for most of women's Acquired Selves. They compare each other's appearance, clothes, jewelry, etc. They constantly judge each other's looks and appearances.

A nice compliment can make us feel on top of the world: a momentary thrill. Then of course, we want more of it. That means spending more time and money on our looks.

A negative comment, on the other hand, rips us apart, makes us sad and sometimes even revengeful. We get so attached to our looks that even a slight reminder of reality, such as a pimple or a weight gain of a few pounds, throws us in a downward spin and creates huge anxiety.

The Concepts of Romance And Marriage

Our growing Acquired Self also acquires concepts of romance and marriage, starting from a young age. All those storybooks and movies about princes and princesses, and later, TV shows, movies, and books about romance feed into our developing Acquired Self.

We also start to learn about dating games in our early teens. To find our mate, we start to compete. In dances and parties, there is intense competition for mates, sometimes resulting in verbal and even physical fights.

Every now and then we get lucky. As a male, as soon as you can have sex, you have conquered, won the game and you are no longer interested. Now, you are on to the next hunt while she is chasing you. You are the winner, and she is the loser. You're feeling high while she's feeling hurt and low. Your excitement is usually short lived. Sooner or later, you fall in love with a girl, and now she may dump you. Now she is the winner, and you are the loser.

Or it may be that you are homosexual, but the game of dating is usually the same: aimed at finding a sexual partner which often turns into a lot of emotional drama.

After playing this game of "win and lose" a few times, people start looking for a serious relationship and some may get married.

In some cultures, the Society Monster has assigned the task of finding a bride or groom to the parents. Now it's the parents who go through intense scrutiny (comparison) while selecting a bride or groom for their son or daughter.

The Honeymoon Is Over

In the case of marriage (or a long-term relationship), there is an initial period of excitement which is usually short-lived. Then, the monster in each one of us starts to act out. All of the piled-up anger, humiliation, abandonment, sadness, jealousy, and "need to win" starts to surface. Arguments and fights become routine. Romantic love withers away.

Compromise

You may get tired of stressful romantic relationships and try to find some solution. People often turn to society for help and may seek marriage counselors (or the elders in some cultures). The usual advice is "to compromise," which may push down irritations, frustrations and anger temporarily. However, the root cause of stress, the Acquired Self, continues to thrive.

Self-Pity

In the meantime, if we also have a child or two, our selfishness may get further enhanced. We may start to feel that we are working hard for everyone else and have no time for ourselves to do the things that we want to do. Life seems so meaningless and boring. We start to feel sorry for ourselves.

Working Like A Machine

We go to work where everything is routine and stressful: customers, colleagues and bosses are so demanding. We are basically trying to survive all day long. Then, we face the stress of rush hour traffic. Finally, we get home but are exhausted, often with a headache. Then, we also must deal with our spouse, kids, and our household responsibilities.

One of us must take the kids to school, keep the house, and prepare meals as well. Usually, it is a female, working to be a career woman, raising a family and trying to be a super mom. However, it is changing now. More men are getting involved in the daily chores of housekeeping.

Morning time is often very stressful because school starts on time. Our Acquired Self has learned that there will be consequences if our kid is not on time. Unfortunately, our kid's Acquired Self hasn't grasped the whole concept yet. Without being aware, we start yelling at our kids for being late again. Soon, they start to yell back. Now, we are really enraged. "Don't talk to me in that tone, young lady!"

We also must show up at work on time. Most people encounter morning rush hour: bumper to bumper traffic. Scared of the consequences of being late (may lose our job), we feel rushed and anxious. We may easily explode in anger if some other driver doesn't behave according to our expectations, which arise out of the traffic rules embedded in our Acquired Self.

One of us also must take our kids to after-school and weekend activities. We feel obligated to enroll our kids in these activities because they are good for our kids, says the Society Collective Acquired Self. These activities start on time and often we are rushed to make it on time. Under stress, parents and kids start yelling at each other. Then, we are in a bad mood by the time we reach the playground.

If our team loses, the kids feel sad and humiliated and sometime even start crying. As a loving parent, we also endure all these pains. Next time, when our team wins, it is the kids and parents on the other side of the field who experience sadness. However, our Acquired Self does not think about them. It tells us to celebrate our victory and be happy.

At home, we get easily annoyed at the demands of our kids and spouse. Finally, our inner irritation cannot take it anymore and we yell at them over little annoyances.

Guilt

Then we feel bad and guilty about it. Why? Because Society's Collective Acquired Self has written a "book of role descriptions." It describes our role as a husband, wife, partner, parent, and child and downloads it into our developing Acquired Self at a relatively young age. If we do our role by the book, society judges us to be a good husband, wife, partner, father, or mother. Otherwise, we are a bad husband, wife, partner, or parent. Often, there is a conflict between how we are supposed to act (according to the book) and how we really behave. Then, we regret what we said or did. This is the basis of guilt.

Sometimes, circumstances are such that we are unable to act according to the book, which also leads to guilt.

Guilt is a gnawing pain that you often suffer from alone. You cannot even talk to your friends or family members about it because you are afraid that they will judge you to be a bad person.

Unresolved guilt often leads to sadness, and even depression and suicide.

Emptiness

We are afraid to even tell anyone how we truly feel about our spouse, children, or elderly parents because we are afraid others will judge us. We feel isolated and lonely. No one seems to understand us. We are constantly irritated. We feel empty inside. We may also feel sad or even depressed due to some guilt.

Escapes

When stress becomes unbearable, we find escapes into excessive work, alcohol, sports, drugs (legal and illegal), gambling, video games, religion, etc.

Most people chase more money. With money, we can buy expensive presents for our spouse, buy a bigger home, buy a more expensive car, or take a trip to an expensive vacation resort. All these activities provide us with a momentary thrill and excitement and boost our ego. However, it fades away fast and then we return to our chronic state of unease, irritation, and emptiness.

To pay for these expensive items, we must work harder. Often, we spend most of our time at work, which we don't like if we are caring parents and want to spend time with our children. This adds to our sense of having no control over our life and deepens our frustration. We start to hate our job.

On the other hand, some people find relief in being away from their family. They mistakenly think their family is the cause of all their problems. Often, they end up having an affair. They find someone who feeds the Acquired Self's hunger for praise and validation. The stress of hiding the affair eventually implodes into a big blow out when their spouse discovers the affair. Often, the end result is a divorce.

Blaming

Now the monstrous Acquired Self in each of us comes out with full force. It is full of hate, anger, and revenge. Each one tries to cause as much harm to the other as possible. Kids are the ones who are in the middle and may suffer the most in the long run. Each one blames the other for all of their problems.

Blaming others is one of the basic features of the Acquired Self. Blaming is a form of judging others. We don't see a problem in our own behavior but are quick to see someone else's faults. Our Acquired Self has learned to never admit any faults, because admitting fault means we're a loser. It may also put us at risk for punishment for our actions.

Stress Of Teenagers

Society's Collective Acquired Self tells parents' Acquired Self to discipline their teenagers with rules. At the same time, it tells teenagers to rebel against the rules. Interesting, isn't it? Society's Collective Acquired Self plays the trick of "Divide and Conquer." In this way, it escapes its own detection and continues to thrive in parents and their children. Ironically, neither parents nor teenagers see the tricks of Society's Collective Acquired Self, the mastermind behind the friction between parents and teenagers.

Our Acquired Self and our teenager's Acquired Self continue to tangle with each other, leading to frustrations, disappointments, and anger.

Often, we go through a couple of relationships and divorces before we settle down in a long relationship, which often requires another role for us - the role of stepparent. Often, step-parenting creates a host of new emotional challenges, centered around control issues as well as jealousy.

The Empty Nest Syndrome

Then, one day our children leave the house. Now, we may suffer from what Society's Collective Acquired Self calls "Empty Nest Syndrome." What really happened is that we treated our children as possessions and now we don't have that possession and control any more. We feel sad.

Children also satisfy our desire to be needed, which boosts our ego as someone important: Someone who provides food, clothes, toys, and transportation. Someone who pays for birthday parties, various enrollment expenses, and other school expenses.

Once our children are gone, we are not that important anymore. We feel worthless and sad.

Children also serve as a distraction from our own deep seated emotional pains. With our children gone, we are faced with the demons stored in our memory box, which is part of the Acquired Self.

Over The Hill Syndrome

Now we have entered middle age. Society's Acquired Self has already downloaded a bleak picture into our personal Acquired Self. We hear phrases like" You're over the hill," "Not hot anymore."

Every morning, the mirror reminds us, our looks are fading away. Our children don't need us anymore. We start to feel worthless and depressed.

Fear

The Society Monster also forecasts a future in which we lose our health. Fear of losing our health is immense. In addition, there may be fear of losing our job, our house, or our stock portfolio, etc.

If our child dates someone we don't approve of, we may also develop fear of losing our child.

Medical Diseases

At this stage of our life, we usually suffer from several chronic medical diseases, such as high blood pressure, diabetes, heart disease, anxiety, and depression, all of which are created by our emotional stress, unhealthy eating habits, sedentary lifestyle, lack of adequate sleep. All are created by our own Acquired Self, but we don't realize it (neither do our doctors).

Instead of looking deeper, we follow the advice of Society's Collective Acquired Self and consult medical doctors who conveniently prescribe various medications. Before you know it, we are on a long list of medications, each one loaded with serious side-effects.

Society's Collective Acquired Self also advises us to fight our disease whether it be cancer, diabetes, or heart disease. So, we put up a wall of resistance without realizing we are fighting our own body.

Society's Collective Acquired Self also tells our Acquired Self that we can cheat death. It implies that medical technology can make us live forever. However, when reality hits and someone close to us dies, we become angry at doctors and fearful of our own death.

Hope

Society's Collective Acquired Self also creates a future for us that promises will be better than the present. We call it "hope."

Retirement

It blames most of our stress on our job and promises us "golden years" after retirement. We'll have no responsibilities and can travel the world and have as much fun as we want.

However, we stay in the grip of our Acquired Self no matter where we are. For example, we may be sitting at the location of our dream vacation, but we continue to be enslaved by comparison, competition, and judging, creating a big cloud of negativity wherever we go.

After retirement, our dream of golden years may be shaken when we (or our spouse) are diagnosed with some serious, incurable illness. We feel cheated. "What did I do to get in this mess and how can I get out of it?" We become regular visitors to doctors and hospitals. We want our health back, but often it is not possible. We get bitter at the system, the government, and even God.

Fear of Poverty, Disability And Death

At this late stage in our life, society considers us useless, an economic burden, and even makes jokes about us.

In our retired life, most of us are living on a budget. A great deal of our money is eaten up by the cost of drugs, doctors, and hospitals bills. We become afraid we may not have enough money left to take care of our lifestyle. For the same reason, many of us may decide *not* to retire, even though it might be quite challenging to continue our job. Some of us get so attached to our career that it becomes our identity, albeit false, but we don't realize it. For instance, a doctor may think he will be nobody if he retires.

We may read horrible stories about diseases and disabilities of old age. We may read (or hear) stories of nursing homes and get scared. Thoughts like "What if I end up in a nursing home" make us shiver inside. We may also read (or hear) some horrible story about someone dying a miserable death from cancer, which makes us even more fearful. "What if that happens to me?" An inner voice pops up and robs us of our sleep.

We may hear (or read) how an elderly person became a big burden to their family. (This happens in countries where there are no nursing homes.)

Attending funerals of friends and family members becomes our frequent activity. Each funeral service reminds us of our own death.

In this way, our Acquired self continues to make us very afraid of poverty, diseases, disability, and death.

It's our Acquired Self who's afraid of dying and wants to live forever. It continues to generate fear of death for us. Then one day, reality hits and we are gone from this world. In this way, we waste our precious life worrying about death, which eventually will arrive for us all one day.

Unfortunately, we carry all emotional burden on our soul. Perhaps if there is reincarnation, our emotionally burdened soul starts its new journey in a newborn baby who may start to exhibit signs of carried over emotional distress at an early stage of life.

More on it in my book,

"Wake Up While You Can"

The Acquired Self Continues To Live On!

We are dead, but our Acquired Self has skillfully perpetuated itself through our children, who carry on our Acquired Self with the special blend of their own Acquired Self. Then, they download all their Acquired Self into their children, and those children repeat it in their children. In this way, the Acquired Self continues to live on, and the drama of stress created by it goes on forever!

CHAPTER: 7

INSTILLATION OF INFORMATION

Society's Collective Acquired Self also instills tons of more concepts in the form of information into our developing Acquired Self.

This Is Your Religion

At birth we have no religion. No baby comes out in the world and announces, "I am a Christian," or "I am a Muslim," or "I am a Hindu," etc.

It is our parents (and grandparents) who gradually download their religious beliefs into our growing Acquired Self. As grownups, we completely forget that we had no religion at birth. Instead, we identify ourselves as Christians, Muslims, Hindus, etc.

At birth, we are all connected as human beings but as grownups we are divided into Christians, Muslims, Hindus, etc.

This Is Your Nationality

Our parents, grandparents and teachers gradually download the concept of citizenship: "You are Canadian," "You are Indian," "You are British," "You are American," etc.

This concept has a functional value for living in the human conceptual world. However, as grownups we start to believe ourselves to be Canadian, Indian, British, American, etc. In this way, we are further divided into groups.

This Is Your Race And Ethnicity

Society's Collective Acquired Self has also created concepts of race and ethnicities, which gets downloaded into our Acquired Self.

As a grownup, we often start to believe that we are Caucasian, Latino, Black, Native American, Asian, etc.

In this way, we are further divided into groups.

This Is Your Culture

Our parents, grandparents and their social network instill into our growing Acquired Self their language, foods, traditions, ceremonies, customs, and expected behavior.

Our parents reinforce their cultural and religious ideas by taking us to churches, temples, mosques, or other cultural places, and celebrating religious and cultural holidays.

This is Your History

Parents, teachers, religious and cultural leaders also download the knowledge of history (from their own perspective) into our growing Acquired Self.

History is often laden with stories of battles and wars between various groups of people. Each group has their own version of the same event. These stories are filled with glory and pride if our ancestors won the war. There are even some kind of justifications if our ancestors killed thousands of innocent people. On the other hand, if our ancestors were victims, the stories are filled with sadness, unfairness, hate, grievances, and revenge.

Us Against Them

The concepts of religion, nationality, race, ethnicity, and culture divide us into groups, while at birth, we are all human beings. As grownups, our Acquired Selves unite us with those who have the same concepts of religion, nationality, race, ethnicity, or culture and divide us from those who don't have the same concepts. This is the basis of "Us Against Them," which has been the basis of human conflicts since the dawn of civilization.

Collective Ego

The concepts of religion, nationality, race, ethnicity, and culture also create a collective ego for that group of individuals. As a grown-up, your Acquired Self makes you feel "special" because you belong to a certain religion, nationality, race, ethnicity, or culture.

This Is What You Must Know

Our parents, grandparents, and society's leaders download their personal stories into our growing Acquired Self. These stories are often laden with exaggerations, heroism, prejudices, fear, anger, and hate.

You Must Acquire

More and More Knowledge.

At schools, we are forced to read and acquire as much information as possible. Our fun and play time start to decline as we advance through school. Initially, we don't like it. "What happened to all the play and fun I used to have?" However, teachers and parents skillfully use the "reward and punishment" strategy to tame us and often succeed in their mission.

Don’t Blame Your Parents or Teachers

Don’t blame your parents or teachers for instilling information into your Acquired Self. They do so with good intentions. In their hearts, they believe they’re doing you good. They’re preparing you to be a responsible and productive citizen of society, as well as to become a successful person with a lot of money and fame.

An Insatiable Appetite for Information

By the time you grow up, your Acquired Self has developed an insatiable appetite for information. It wants to be the first one to know the latest sensational stories and it doesn’t want to miss out on any gossip.

So, it starts its day feeding itself a healthy breakfast by checking the headlines, emails, weather forecast, entertainment, etc. while scrolling on a smart phone, watching TV, or reading articles.

For the rest of the day, it continues to use a Smart phone, TV, and colleagues as a source for its food.

Then, it makes sure to feed itself a good dinner in the form of news updates, emails, online videos, etc. before going to bed.

Opinions Become Truth

Information in the form of stories, concepts, ideas, and beliefs becomes an important part of the Acquired Self. Often, we don't even realize that most of this information is basically the opinions of others. Often, we start to believe all this secondhand information to be the "truth." Then we look at the world through the filters of this acquired information.

Consequently, most of our experiences are tainted by those preconceived notions. Hence, we don't have any original experiences!

For example, when we look at someone, we instantaneously judge that person, based upon the information in our head without even exchanging a word. This is the basis of prejudice.

Another example: We may hear about a country. Soon, we regurgitate all the information we have heard about that country including its people, culture, and history although we may have never been there and haven't met anyone from that country or culture. Amazing!

Sometimes two people may even take mental positions and start arguing, each one believing that his information is true and the other person's information is not. This can lead to bad feelings, verbal violence, and sometimes even physical violence.

Academic Knowledge

At schools, our Acquired Self continues to eat up a lot of knowledge in the form of science, liberal arts, business, law, medicine, etc. Then one day, we graduate as doctor, engineer, lawyer, etc. Unfortunately, that label becomes part of our Acquired Self. Most of us forget that it is just a profession: our means to make a living as well as trying to help other people, animals, and plants etc.

CHAPTER: 8

CREATION OF THE PAST AND FUTURE

"Past and future" are major components of the Acquired Self. What is "past and future"? Use logic and you will realize that whatever happened in the past is not happening right now. Whatever may happen in the so-called future is not happening right now. The past is dead and gone and the future never arrives. Hence, both are virtual and unreal in the Now.

Just like a monster, the past and future are virtual, but they each have huge power over you. They may seem real, but in fact they are not. Can you show me your past or future? Of course not! Even old videos or photos are images, not reality.

The past was real when it happened, but it is not happening right now. Hence, it is unreal in the Now. The future never happens. When it happens, it happens in the Now. The past and future are nothing but mental abstractions. Both are created by the mind.

How Our Mind Creates Past And Future

For a while, I used to ponder over the question: How does the mind create "the past and future"? Then one day, the answer just struck me, when I wasn't even thinking about it.

I was sitting in my backyard looking at the sky, clouds, birds, flowers, and trees and feeling the breeze. Then a friend of mine visited me. We had a chat for 15-20 minutes and then he left. About five minutes later, I had a flashback of my friend's visit. I could hear him calling my name, coming and sitting on the chair next to mine. I could recall our conversation, and I vividly remember his departure. The whole event was as fresh in my mind as if it was happening right now.

I had a realization that truly transformed me. I realized that my friend's visit was an event, with a beginning and an ending. However, my mind took a mental picture of it, attached the whole conversation as a story and judged it as a good experience. This triggered the emotion of happiness and the entire bundle of picture, story, mental judging and the provoked emotion was stored as "My sweet memory." It became part of "My Acquired Self." Now, "I" can go back to it any time "I" want and experience the whole event over and over again. That's how the event is kept alive, although the event has ended.

Events happen all the time. The mind continues to make mental pictures of events, with attached stories and triggered emotions. It then stores them in the memory box of the Acquired Self. That's how it creates "My Past." With this background, our mind also tries to figure out how the next event is going to be or rather how it should or should not be, which triggers emotions. Often, it also creates mental pictures through imagination. The self-generated thoughts and associated mental pictures is what it calls "My future."

Past And Future Are Unreal

Past and future are all in our heads, aren't they? They are unreal, virtual… a mental abstraction… an illusion. Neither past nor future exists in the reality of Now. **However, to the mind they are real.** Why? Because the mind creates them. How could it not believe in its own creation?

The Busy Mind

Since the mind creates these entities called past and future, it loves to dwell in them. We could call them its home. That's why our mind stays stuck in the so-called past and future. That is why we have such a busy mind.

Medically speaking, the more frequently a network of memory neurons (brain cells) is traveled, the stronger the network of neurons becomes. Then, electrical impulses can run through this circuit of neurons more easily, without much resistance. This is the basis of the "busy mind."

Since the "busy mind" is created by the Acquired Self, we cannot be free of it if we stay in the trap of the Acquired Self.

Stress Created By the "Past and Future"

By keeping the old dead events alive, our busy mind keeps the fire of old emotions burning inside us. It calls them "my past" and "my memories." It judges these memories as either good or bad, which triggers the corresponding good or bad emotions.

Stress Due To Bad Memories

By replaying the bad memories, our busy mind continues to trigger *negative* emotions attached to these memories. These negative emotions can be in the form of humiliation, anger, hate, bitterness, guilt, jealousy, unfairness, and revenge.

Stress Due To Good Memories

When our mind replays good memories, we start to miss those wonderful experiences which make us sad. In this way, even good memories create stress for us.

Acquired Self Wants To Change Its Past.

Here's another interesting phenomenon. Our Acquired Self wants to control the virtual world of memories. It is strongly attached to sweet memories, but it wants to run away from bad memories Therefore, it tries to change the stories and events.

Examples:

- "I wish I had not listened to him."
- "I wish my teacher hadn't humiliated me in front of entire class. Then, I'd be a happy person today."
- "If I didn't trust her, I wouldn't be hurting due to her backstabbing."
- "Why didn't I see the clues? He's been cheating on me all along! I should have dumped him a long time ago."
- "Why did I become a teacher? My principal is so mean and demanding."
- "I wish I had taken some action earlier."
- "I wish I had not insulted him."

But of course, the Acquired Self can't change what has already happened. Therefore, it continues to feel humiliated, disappointed, annoyed, frustrated, angry, and sometimes guilty as well. The more it tries to change those painful memories, the stronger they get. What an irony!

How To Be Free Of Old Emotional Memories

Take the following steps to get rid of the old emotional memories:

1. Realize the more you stay in the memories, the stronger they get. As I mentioned earlier, those networks of brain cells which are traveled frequently, grow stronger. Therefore, do not dwell in emotional memories. No need to change them.
2. Fully realize those emotional memories were created by your own Acquired Self. They serve no purpose. In fact, they prevent you from living freely in the Now.
3. Bad emotional memories are, in fact, harmful for cognitive functions of the brain. This is one of the reasons for dementia.
4. Realize those events absolutely do not exist at this moment. Hence, let them go!

Acquired Self Wants To Secure A Happy Future

Our Acquired Self doesn't want any bad event to ever happen again! It wants perfect security. Why? Because Society's Collective Acquired Self trains our individual Acquired Self to *learn* from the past. Therefore, it wants to create a perfect world for itself in which there are only "good things" and no "bad things." It wants to create a paradise for itself. Therefore, it continues to generate new thoughts along the lines of how to prevent bad events from happening again.

The "What If" Syndrome

But then another thought erupts: "What if it happens again?" That triggers huge fear and anxiety.

Caught up in the "what if, what may, what will I do syndrome," the Acquired Self creates a virtual, never-ending movie. In this way, it creates a perpetual fear for us. In the pursuit of security and peace, our Acquired Self robs us of any peace we have. How counter-productive!

EXAMPLES:

- "What if I lose my job again?"
- "What if I get a bad grade again?"
- "What if I get dumped again?"

- "What if I get stung by the bee again?"
- "What if my boyfriend/girlfriend cheats on me, again?"
- "What if my students make fun of me again?"
- "What if I lose my friend again?"
- "What if I'm late again?"
- "What if I miss my flight again?"
- "What if no one pays attention to me again?"
- "What if my wife cheats on me again?"
- "What if my principle insults me again?"
- "What if I become fat again?"
- "What if I have an attack of asthma again?"

Society's Collective Acquired Self reinforces this syndrome of "what if, what may, what will I do" in the form of information conveyed by newspapers, books, TV and the internet. It teaches us to learn from the past. In this way, the busy mind inside us –our Acquired Self – keeps generating huge amounts of fear and anxiety.

The Expansion Of Past And Future

In addition to personal experiences, our Acquired Self also borrows experiences of others and considers them as its own.

For example, as a parent we may read or hear stories about some teenager who got killed by another teenager or who got addicted to drugs and quit high school, or who got pregnant and dumped by her boyfriend. Our mind creates an image, attaches the provided story, judges it to be bad (which triggers bad emotions) and the entire bundle gets stored in our memory box. The Acquired Self then generates another thought: “This must never happen to my teenager!” Then another thought pops up: “But what if…?” And we may end up having an anxiety attack.

As teenagers, we may hear stories about hardships for people who didn’t go to college. Our Acquired Self stores all these experiences of others into our memory box. The Acquired Self then creates another thought: "What if I can’t get into college?" This kind of thought creates huge anxiety.

Now consider how often we read stories in books, magazines and newspapers. Add to that the stories we watch on TV, the internet and movies. Obviously, these are the experiences of people we have never even met. Some stories happened thousands of miles away or many centuries ago. Many are not even real experiences, but simple fiction. However, our Acquired Self clings to those experiences of the others (real or fictional) as if they were our own experiences. That adds a lot of stress in our life.

Collective Human Past

Every Society’s Collective Acquired Self creates its own virtual past and a virtual future. It likes to dwell in its past, which it calls “Our history.” Then, society makes sure the knowledge of its history is downloaded into everyone growing up in that society.

Everyone believes this downloaded information to be accurate without realizing that it is simply someone's (the historian's) point of view. Obviously, these stories are tainted by the historian's own Acquired Self. That's why there are so many conflicting stories about the same event or figure in the collective human past. Often, one set of stories has been downloaded in the Acquired Self of people in one group. Meanwhile, another conflicting set of stories is downloaded into the Acquired Self of another group of people. Collectively, people in each group believe their story to be true because their Acquired Self identifies with their Collective Acquired Self of their religion, culture, nationality, etc.

Often these stories perpetuate hate, grievances, and revenge and sometimes can lead to verbal or physical violence and even battles and wars.

Collective Human Future

The Collective Acquired Self of a group of people learns from its (or even others) collective past. Basically, what it learns is that the "powerful" group of people has tremendous advantage over the "weak" group of people. Therefore, it wants to be as powerful as it can. In this way, it tries to secure a future for its people in which everything is good and nothing bad ever happens. This is the basis of the "Pursuit of Power" since the dawn of civilization.

The Collective Acquired Self of our religion, culture, country, etc. wants us to never forget its past and therefore continues to propagate hate, grievances, and revenge. It also creates "what if, what may, and what should we do" syndrome. In this way, it spreads fear and anxiety about the so-called tomorrow. It creates hypothetical fearful situations for us and then tells us how we should prepare ourselves to deal with the frightening situations as if they were happening right now.

In the grip of fear, we lose our common sense and start to believe in the narrative of the Collective Acquired Self, no matter how untruthful, unreasonable and ridiculous it may be. This is one way Society's Collective Acquired Self keeps us under its tight control.

Emotional Memory

Versus

Cognitive Memory

What we have observed so far is what we can call "Emotional Memory." In addition, there is another type of memory, which is cognitive in nature.

For example, memorizing information and knowledge such as mathematical, scientific or geographic knowledge. This type of memory, "Cognitive Memory," is non-emotional.

Cognitive memory is useful and helps us to function in society. In fact, our brain functions much better when we are free of emotional meddling.

Thinking with a "cool head" is much more productive than thinking with a "hot head."

EXAMPLES:

- We can solve a difficult problem when we are free of fear and anger.
- We become better drivers when we are not lost in our emotional memory.
- We become better doctors when we are not worried about lawsuits or angry over something in the past.
- We become better waiters at a restaurant when we are not worried about our job or angry over something in the past.
- We become better players when we are not worried about the outcome or sad over something in the past.
- As students, we earn a better score when we are not worried about the grade or upset over something in the past.

In short, non-emotional memory makes us function better in society. On the other hand, emotional memory interferes with our true potential.

Emotional Memory Causes Forgetfulness.

In addition to all the emotional stress, emotional memory also causes memory loss. How ironic! Observe yourself. Next time, you are angry or fearful, you may not remember where you put your keys, wallet, or phone.

Emotional memory gradually makes a person more forgetful. In this way, emotional memory decreases a person's ability for cognitive thinking and memory. In other words, the fire of emotions slowly burns down the entire chamber of memory. In my opinion, this is a major reason for dementia.

CHAPTER: 9

COMPOSITION OF THE ACQUIRED SELF

At the core of our Acquired Self is the virtual, conceptual "I," we mistakenly think we are. Around this "I," there are layers and layers of concepts, information, past and future, emotional thoughts, and triggered emotions.

The Virtual "I"

The virtual "I" becomes the owner of the concepts, information, objects, people, animals, past, and future.

Some examples:

- My concepts
- My beliefs
- My traditions
- My school
- My knowledge
- My money
- My career
- My goals
- My car

- My house
- My husband
- My girlfriend
- My beauty
- My jewelry
- My ancestors
- My accomplishments
- My failures
- My job
- My relationships
- My values
- My ambitions
- My culture
- My town
- My country
- My land
- My religion
- My past
- My future

Emotional Thoughts

Looking through the filters of downloaded concepts, beliefs, dogmas, rules, and information, the Virtual "I" interprets and judges every event, every person, every object, etc.

In addition, it roams in the “dead valley” of the past and leaps into the “virtual cloud” of the future, skillfully keeping us away from the peaceful, real land of the Now. Consequently, it creates a busy mind loaded with emotional thoughts.

Emotional Stress

Every emotional thought triggers a corresponding emotion. For example, an angry thought will trigger anger, a fearful thought will trigger fear, an exciting thought will trigger excitement etc. In this way, emotional thoughts create a huge amount of emotional stress for us.

Emotional stress takes the form of fear, anger, annoyances, irritations, restlessness, agitation, thrills, excitement, hate, grievances, unfairness, revenge, conditional love, boredom, loneliness, worthlessness, sadness, depression, guilt, self-pity, grief, etc.

Emotional Actions

Often actions arise out of our emotional thoughts, which cause more stress for us as well as others.

In Short

The Virtual “I” lies at the core of the Acquired Self. It is surrounded by layers of more concepts, beliefs, dogmas, rules, information, past, and future. Using these filters, it interprets and judges every event, every person, every object, which triggers emotions. In turn, emotions create more emotional thoughts and a busy mind ensues.

Emotional thoughts often give rise to emotional actions which create more emotional stress and a never-ending vicious cycle of emotional thoughts – emotions – emotional actions – emotional thoughts – emotions – emotional actions.

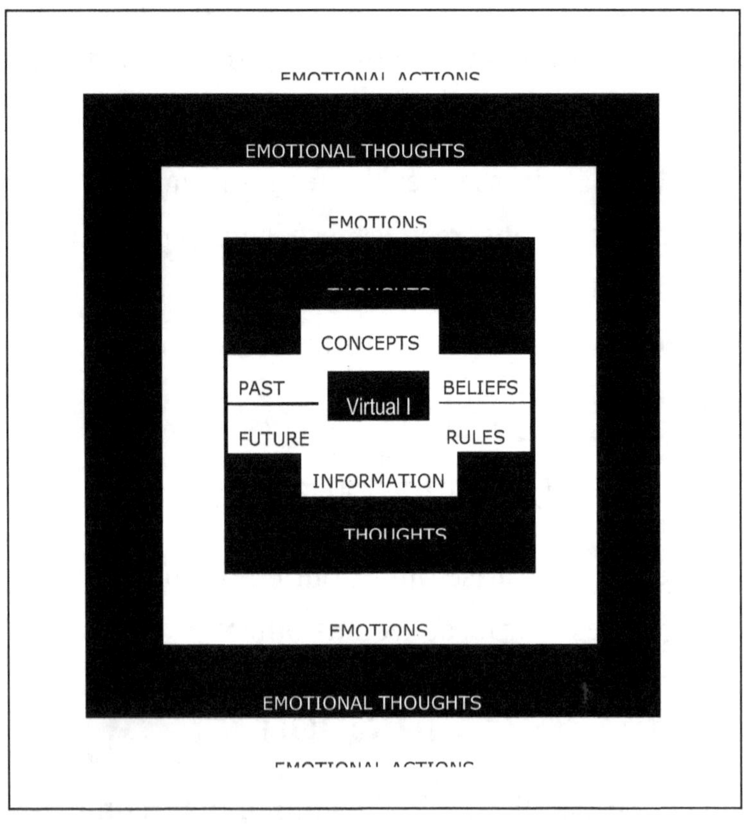

Acquired Self

Section 2

The Collective Acquired Self

CHAPTER: 10

THE COLLECTIVE ACQUIRED SELF

In addition to the "Individual Acquired Self" we also have the "Collective Acquired Self," which we call society.

The "Individual Acquired Self" is a product of the "Collective Acquired Self." In turn, the "Individual Acquired Self" feeds the "Collective Acquired Self." In this way, "the Individual Acquired Self" and "the Collective Acquired Self" are interconnected, bouncing off each other, and feeding each other.

Societies collectively give rise to what we call the "Human World."

Let's take a closer look at this "Human World," using our common sense.

CHAPTER: 11

A VIRTUAL, CONCEPTUAL WORLD

The human world which is created by "the Collective Human Mind" is not real. Why?

The "Human World" is based on concepts. Every concept is virtual. Therefore, the "Human World" is conceptual and virtual.

Imagine a three-year old sitting on a window seat in an airplane while traveling from New York to New Delhi with her parents. That child would see sky, clouds, water, mountains, trees, buildings, roads, humans, etc. However, she wouldn't see London, Paris, Cairo, Dubai, Lahore on the way, but her parents would point them out to her: "There is London, etc."

What is London? A concept attached to a certain part of Planet Earth. That's all. In reality, it is land, sky, clouds, water, trees, humans, buildings, etc. However, in the human world, it is "London," with all its history, language, culture, museums, restaurants, newspapers, etc. So is "Paris" with all its history, language, culture, museums, restaurants, newspapers, etc. So are Cairo, Dubai, Lahore and New Delhi, etc.

In short, the "Human World" is virtual, but we grown-ups accept it as Real. We never question it, but the moment we do, using our simple common sense, it becomes clear that the "Human World" is in fact virtual. However, the actions arising out of the concepts are real with serious consequences.

CHAPTER: 12

A STRESSED-OUT WORLD

Everyone in the "Human World" seems to be stressed-out, don't they? Let's dive deep to figure out why everyone is so stressed out.

As observed earlier, when a baby grows up in society, it acquires societal concepts. Slowly, the child loses their identity to a virtual, false self, we can call the Acquired Self.

The Acquired Self creates emotional stress. With few exceptions, everyone in the "Human World" is in the grip of their Acquired Self. That's the reason why the "Human World" is a such a stressed-out place.

CHAPTER: 13

A FEARFUL WORLD

The Human World is full of fear. Countries are afraid of other countries. Races and religions are afraid of other races and religions. Political parties are afraid of each other. Businesses are afraid of each other. With few exceptions, every person lives in fear.

Have you ever pondered over it? Why is everyone so fearful, (although on the surface they may claim to be fearless)?

Basis Of Fear

To figure out why everyone is fearful, we need to dig deeper with common sense.

Fear comes from perceived threat, which is virtual, not real. In other words, your conditioned mind – The Acquired Self – is thinking about a potential threat and worries about it. This is the basis of "What If Thinking."

Examples:

- What if I lose my smart phone?
- What if I lose my credit card?
- What if I lose my job?
- What if I miss my flight?
- What if I lose my dog
- What if I lose my identity?
- What if I lose my looks?
- What if I lose my car?
- What if I lose my wife?
- What if I lose my business?
- What if I lose my health?
- What if I lose my life?
- What if I get stuck in the elevator?
- What if I can't find a job?
- What if I can't find a boyfriend?
- What if I don't pass the exam?
- What if I develop cancer?
- What if I lose my autonomy?
- What if I lose my house?

- What if I lose my professional license?
- What if I get thrown in jail by mistake?
- What if I lose my immigration status?
- What If I get caught?
- What If My party loses elections?
- What If My country loses the war?
- What If My religion is attacked?
- What If My sports team loses its game?
- What If people make fun of Me?

If you pay attention, you realize that there are two essential components in the thought process that creates fear.

1. "I, Me, My, Mine"

2. A hypothetical situation, which "I" perceives as a threat.

Let's take a closer look at the "I." It's your Acquired Self, isn't it?

Fear is created by your Acquired Self to protect itself. When you identify with your Acquired Self, obviously you feel this fear. In the grip of your Acquired Self, you will continue to stay fearful.

As most people stay in the grip of their Acquired Self, there is much fear in the Human World.

Each Acquired Self contains a lot of concepts such as concepts of wealth, beauty, possessions, profession, family, health, nationality, religion, culture, etc. To survive, it must protect these concepts. Any thought that it may lose any of its components obviously creates a virtual threat which creates fear.

Your Acquired Self does not want to ever lose anything or anyone that is "Mine." That's why it looks for security, which does not exist.

The more possessions you have as "Mine," the more you fear losing them, and the more you try to protect them. As a result, you stay very fearful. For example, as a wealthy person, you may end up living in a gated community to protect your belongings. You may become a frequent visitor to a plastic surgeon to preserve your looks.

I have seen patients wanting to be seen on an urgent basis because they noticed hair falling out of their head during their shower that morning. They are panicked, as if it's the end of the world.

Dynamics Of Fear

Now, let's examine how your Acquired Self uses experiences and information to create fear for itself.

Your mind (your Acquired Self) creates a mental picture of every experience. It doesn't matter if it's a real experience (your own experience) or a virtual experience (someone else's experience that you see on a screen or read about in a book).

The “Acquired Self” judges each experience as happy or sad, good or bad, pleasurable or painful according to the conditioning of the mind, based on past experiences and stored information from stories, newspapers, books, magazines, TV or the internet. After judging, it stores the experience in the memory box where it stays alive, even years later.

Your Acquired Self gets very attached to good, happy and pleasurable experiences such as memories associated with happiness, position, power, fame, success, and victories. It wants more of these experiences. It does not want to lose them ever. Even the idea of losing them creates fear. For example, even the idea of losing photos of your sweet memories will create huge amount of fear.

In addition, your Acquired Self wants to avoid unpleasant experiences such as those associated with failure, punishment, loneliness, humiliation, poverty, and disease, etc. Even the thought of unpleasant experiences triggers intense fear.

It’s interesting to note that your Acquired Self reacts to “hypothetical situations” that it creates itself. Pretty crazy, isn’t it? Those situations don’t exist at all. It creates a threatening hypothetical situation and then tries to solve it. As the threat is hypothetical, so are all the solutions. Your Acquired Self is so insecure and so afraid of its own death, that it creates all possible dreadful scenarios and tries to figure out how it can escape its death in every possible way. In doing so, it keeps the virtual threat alive. How ironic! In this way, your Acquired Self creates tons of unnecessary fear for itself. When you totally identify with your Acquired Self, you experience all this fear.

Isn't Fear Good for Us?

There is a myth that it's natural to be afraid because we have a "fight or flight" response embedded in us. It helps us to survive. It may even be good for us.

Let's take a close look at this concept using common sense, the true intelligence in all human beings.

What happens when you are faced with a real threat? Let's say you're walking through a forest and suddenly, you're face to face with a bear. You take immediate action without thinking. As there is no time for thinking, there is no fear. Instantaneously, you either fight or run away. This intelligence resides in your body. It prepares you instantaneously by releasing a large amount of adrenaline (and noradrenaline) in the blood stream, which increases your heart rate, blood pressure and blood glucose, opens your airways and tenses up your muscles. You are physically *primed* to fight or run away. This is the so-called Fight or Flight response, which happens *instantaneously* and *spontaneously* when you are faced with a *real* threat.

With this immediate action by your innate intelligence, you have a good chance of surviving… Or you may die, becoming food for the bear. In either case, there is no fear.

Let's presume you survived the situation. A few moments later, you start thinking: "What could have happened? I could have died or lost a leg and be paralyzed for the rest of my life. If I had died, what would have happened to my wife and kids?" Now intense fear sets in.

At the time of the actual threatening situation, there was no fear, but thinking about it creates fear.

It's the action at the time of the threatening situation that may save your life. So, it is not fear, but your spontaneous action in a situation that may save your life.

Fear Actually Harms Your Body

The entire experience of facing the bear and your conditioned mind's interpretation and reaction gets stored in your memory box and becomes added to your Acquired Self.

Let's say a month later, you tell your story to a friend. It is basically your memory box repeating the stored event. Even though there is no bear in front of you, your conditioned mind sees a bear and warns your body of this virtual threat. Obviously, there is a big difference between the *real* bear and the *virtual* bear. However, your body cannot distinguish between a real and virtual threat. It relies on your brain that in turn, relies on your mind. So, if your mind sees a threat, so does your body.

Therefore, your body responds to this virtual threat the same way as it did to the real threat: by releasing excessive amounts of adrenaline (and noradrenaline). Your heart starts pounding, blood pressure rises and blood glucose rises. In addition, you also think "what might have happened" and this thinking creates a lot of fear. The net result: you have an unpleasant sensation of fear and physical symptoms of your heart pounding, a rise in blood pressure and blood sugar. Of course, your friends also join in with various thoughts of "what could have happened." They may tell you about a similar story they saw on a screen or read in an article. From these collective thoughts, you all build up a massive "cloud of fear."

Now here is another interesting fact: Since you can neither fight nor flee this virtual situation, the situation does not resolve. Your body continues to release excessive amounts of adrenaline (and noradrenaline). In addition, it also releases excessive amounts of cortisol into blood circulation. Both adrenaline (and noradrenaline) and cortisol (in excessive amounts) have devastating effects on your health as described below.

You will continue to experience fear and its damaging effects on the body as long as you have fearful thoughts. There is no resolution of the situation.

After tormenting you for a while, your Acquired Self (your memory and thoughts) settles down, ready to be awakened each time you talk or think about your frightening experience.

Harmful Effects Of Fear

Repeated episodes of fear cause excess release of adrenaline (and noradrenaline) and cortisol from your adrenal glands, which can lead to high blood pressure, damage to blood vessels, high blood glucose, weight gain (especially fat storage), and a dysfunctional immune system. Then one day, your doctor may diagnose you with hypertension, Type 2 diabetes, fatty liver, coronary artery disease, carotid artery disease, dementia or cancer.

If you already have heart disease, a flashback of a dreadful experience with a rush of adrenaline (and noradrenaline) may cause an acute heart attack. Similarly, if you already have carotid artery disease, an acute rush of adrenaline (and noradrenaline) may cause an acute stroke.

Chronic high adrenal state also increases your risk of migraine headaches, nausea, dizziness, hypersensitivity to sounds, smells, and diarrhea or constipation (IBS: Irritable Bowel Syndrome).

Fear also plays a major role in causing **Autoimmune Diseases** including:

- Asthma,
- Hashimoto's Thyroiditis,
- Graves' Disease,
- Type 1 Diabetes,
- Crohn's Disease,
- Ulcerative Colitis,
- Multiple Sclerosis,
- Lupus,
- Rheumatoid Arthritis.

How Fear May Cause Autoimmune Diseases

Let me explain how fear causes Autoimmune Diseases. What is an autoimmune disease in the first place? Auto-immune means that your own immune system has gone crazy and is attacking your own organs as if they are alien and don't belong in your body. If your immune system attacks your lungs, you develop Asthma. If it attacks your pancreas, you develop Type 1 Diabetes… and so forth.

Why does the immune system start to act in this way? Normally, the immune system works to recognize real threats such as invading bacteria or viruses. It then mounts an attack to kill the invading organisms and then goes back to a resting state.

However, if a person stays in the grip of an Acquired Self that is full of fear, then the immune system remains at high alert to fight off the virtual threat. However, there is no one to fight, so it starts to pick fights and destroys whatever organ it perceives as a threat. How ironic! To attain security, it kills its own parts of the body.

Fear Causes Insomnia

Normally, the human brain and body function in a harmonious way that sets up a biological clock. At the crack of dawn, there is a transient surge in a number of hormones, such as cortisol, growth hormone, and adrenaline (and noradrenaline), all of which act to increase your vigor, blood glucose, and blood pressure. In other words, your brain prepares your body to go and do physical work, as our forefathers did for thousands of years.

As the day advances, these hormones go down. After sunset, cortisol is at very low level. With these hormonal changes, we feel tired and go to bed for a restful sleep. This is what endocrinologists call “our diurnal rhythm.” In layman’s terms, it is our biological clock.

Our modern lifestyle is obviously in conflict with our biological clock. Most people don't wake up at the crack of dawn and don't go to bed hours after sunset. In the evening hours, most people watch TV or surf the internet. Most of this activity centers around fear, sensationalism and excitement, which results in a surge of adrenaline (and noradrenaline) and cortisol. In addition, the brain does not produce enough melatonin, a hormone it produces when our eyes see darkness of the night. All these factors obviously result in a wound-up mind that does not want to shut down. The result is insomnia.

Freedom From Insomnia

Often, people seek advice for their insomnia from a physician who conveniently prescribes a sleeping pill, which forces sleep by causing chemical changes in the brain. However, these pills have serious side-effects, such as daytime somnolence, fatigue, dizziness, lack of coordination, increased risk of accidents, decrease in cognition, memory loss, and dementia. Furthermore, these pills are addictive.

In addition, neither you nor your physician look at the root cause of insomnia. The efficacy of this band-aid approach is often short-lived. With the passage of time, these pills don't work as effectively as they did in the beginning. Then, you end up with higher doses and even multiple medications with many side-effects.

Once you have an insight into the whole mechanics of insomnia and see how your Acquired Self is at the root of your insomnia, you may decide to be free of your Acquired Self. Then, in the evening, you won't have the urge to watch TV or surf the internet. Instead, you might watch the sunset, the stars, and moon. You become aware of the "silence and stillness" of the night. Insomnia automatically vanishes.

Fear Causes Chemical Changes In The Brain

Since your early childhood, your Acquired Self continues to accumulate fearful stories from movies, video games, fiction books, history lessons, etc. It also tightly holds on to its own fearful experiences. Every day it adds more fearful experiences of itself and others from books, TV and the internet. In this way, the Acquired Self creates an ever increasing "tower of fear."

Over time, the neuronal network of fear gets well established in your brain. Then reading, watching or listening to fearful news can turn on this well-established network. Net result: An incredible amount of fear, which causes chemical changes in your brain.

In the milieu of these chemical changes, all the old fearful experiences become alive, which feed in more fearful thoughts, that leads to more emotions of fear, more chemical changes and subsequently, more fearful thoughts.

Thus, a vicious cycle sets in, and you get consumed by fearful thoughts and emotions of fear, both reinforcing each other.

Fear Causes a Constant State Of Unease And Nervousness

Your body responds to the constant bombardment of fearful thoughts and produces an excess release of adrenaline (and noradrenaline). Consequently, many people get in a constant state of unease, nervousness, hyperactivity, restlessness, and agitation. This is commonly known as *nervous energy*, which can help you to accomplish a lot of tasks.

Often, these people can't sit still. They must keep moving, keep doing, one thing after another. Sometimes, they are not even fully aware of their movements and actions. In general, they become good workers. Employers love them. However, at the end of the day, they are totally exhausted. Then, they look for different ways (usually caffeinated drinks) to boost their energy, all of which have their own negative side-effects. They also often suffer from headaches and insomnia.

Many people get so used to their constant state of "unease and nervousness" that they think it's normal for them and there's nothing they can do about it. Society reinforces it by statement like, "your brain is wired differently."

Fear Causes Anxiety And Panic Attacks

Excess adrenaline (and noradrenaline) causes symptoms of restlessness, agitation, insomnia, sweaty palms, and palpitations. We label these symptoms as Anxiety.

If the root cause of anxiety remains untreated, as is often the case, you start to develop even more severe and dramatic symptoms such as chest tightness, air hunger, heart pounding, lump in the throat, excess perspiration, cold sweaty palms, and a feeling of passing out. These symptoms are labeled as Panic Attacks.

It is interesting to note the symptoms of Panic Attacks are similar to the symptoms of an actual heart attack and some other life-threatening medical conditions such as congestive heart failure or a clot in the lungs. Ironically, knowledge of these serious medical conditions (acquired from the internet) frightens you even more and worsens your Panic Attacks. Obviously, many patients with Panic Attacks end up in the emergency department at a hospital.

Medical Treatment Of

Anxiety And Panic Attacks

Typically, after a physician diagnoses you with anxiety disorder or Panic Attack, you are prescribed an anti-anxiety drug which basically works by changing the chemicals in your brain and often gives you temporary relief of symptoms. However, if the root cause of your anxiety is not treated, your anxiety continues like a smoldering fire ready to erupt into flame with any fearful news.

Most anti-anxiety drugs can cause many side-effects including an addiction to the drug. These drugs work as a band-aid. In time, if the root cause of your anxiety and panic attacks is not treated, you will most likely need higher doses of these medications and often will need to keep adding more of these drugs to cover up the volcano of your anxiety and panic attacks.

Cure For

Anxiety And Panic Attacks

Once you develop the insight that the root cause of nervousness, anxiety, and panic attacks resides inside you – as your Acquired Self - you realize that the cure also resides inside you. The moment you can see your Acquired Self at the root of your anxiety; you can start to be free of it.

Use logic and realize that your own thoughts create a hypothetical situation which can be very frightening. With logic, you realize that it is all in your head. The situation is all hypothetical. It is a ghost, a phantom, an illusion; no more.

Stop watching (or listening to) any sensational, fearful, dramatic news. Don't read books, articles, or stories that harbor fear. Be brave enough to tell your friends that you are not interested in fearful, negative news or stories.

Read this chapter frequently with the firm conviction that you are using Divine Healing Power inside you to cure anxiety and panic attacks. This writing came out of the dimension of Divine Intelligence and has an amazing effect that can weaken your well-established neuronal networks of anxiety and panic attacks.

You may still get into your old habits of the mind and find yourself worrying or having a panic attack. Don't worry! Stay on track and you will eventually get rid of all your fear and its manifestations.

On a personal note, I used to suffer from anxiety and panic attacks, (which ultimately led to my Awakening in the park.)

After the park incident, my anxiety vanished as wisdom sank in. However, after about six months, a panic attack hit me again. One night, while ill with Ulcerative Colitis, I woke up around midnight to take a dose of my medicine. Suddenly, a thought struck me. What if this medicine doesn't work and I die? What will happen to my 10-year-old daughter? Almost immediately, I was in a full panic attack.

In the past, I used to wake my wife up for help. This time, I knew it was a transient storm brought on by fearful thoughts and would soon pass. I called it a "monster" trying to scare me.

I was CERTAIN about it. So, I decided not to call my wife for help. Instead, I talked to this "monster" and said something like this: "Ok, let me see who you are. I am not afraid of you because you are not real. You cannot do me any harm as I am part of the DIVINE."

I was 100% confident about what I said. Almost immediately, my anxiety storm started to subside. That was the last time I had a panic attack and that was about twenty years ago.

Acute Management Of A Panic Attack

During a panic attack, take the following steps immediately:

- Sit down if you can. Try not to be standing.

- Realize that it is a transient situation. It will pass soon. Usually, it takes a couple of minutes. No one dies of a panic attack.
- Have the firm conviction that you are one with the Divine. Hence, you are indestructible. You can say it out loud, “I am a manifestation of the Divine, and nothing can harm me.”
- Repeat what I said to this monster. “Ok, let me see who you are. I am not afraid of you because you are not real. You cannot do me any harm as I am part of the DIVINE.”
- Immediately shift your attention to the Now by using your five senses:
- Touch: Start moving your hands all over your body. Feel different parts of your body such as nose, ear, neck, chest, abdomen, arms and legs. You can also touch another person’s hands or arms if feasible.
- Vision: See the objects around you and be aware of the space in which they exist. Watch movements around you. Also be aware of stillness in which all movements take place.
- Hearing: Listen to sounds around you and be aware of the silence which gives rise to sounds. You may decide to start singing some soothing song or listen to some relaxing music.

- Taste something such as a cracker, a piece of bread, fruit, whatever is available. Sip some water.
- Smell: pay attention to some fragrances such as flowers, cologne, incense, essential oil, etc.

You will see that slowly your symptoms will subside.

Using this approach, I not only cured my own anxiety and panic attack but also helped hundreds of my patients.

One of my patients asked for my advice, as she was having a lot of anxiety and insomnia. I asked her what kind of thoughts run through her mind. She said, "I worry a lot and I know that worrying is not good for my health, and you've told me that worrying can affect my immune system, but I can't help it. I have tried books, seen psychiatrists and am on anti-anxiety drugs, but nothing is working any longer. I think I need another drug to calm my nerves."

I counseled her about the True Self and Acquired Self and that the freedom from the Acquired Self was the true cure for her anxiety disorder. "But how can I do it? I understand what you are saying, but I keep going back to anxiety," she said.

I gave her an example. "Suppose you have a five-year-old child, and she gets tangled in a thorny bush and starts crying. You rescue her and tell her not to get tangled in that bush. Five minutes later, she is back in that thorny bush. You rescue her again and repeat your advice, don't you?" She replied, "Yes, of course."

I told her, "Each time you find yourself tangled with a fearful thought, get out of it. And yes, five minutes later, you may find yourself lost in some fearful thought again and you simply free yourself again from it.

Your thought tells you that something bad may happen to you or your loved ones. However, ask yourself, "Is it really happening at this very moment?" Keep asking yourself. The answer will almost always be, "No, it's not happening right now."

Then ask yourself, "What's happening now?" Look around and see what's around you: what you see, hear, smell, touch and taste. This is your field of awareness. Stay in it as much as you can and you will be free of fearful thoughts.

Once free of fearful thoughts, you will be free of anxiety as well as insomnia without using any medications. Once you are cured of anxiety, your immune system will also start to work normally again.

However, stay on your medications until you start living like this: Be aware of your thoughts, don't get tangled up with them and live in your field of awareness. It takes a while before you start to live like this. The more you put this practice into everyday living, the more you will stay in your field of awareness. However, if you just talk about it and don't put it into your daily living, it won't work. In that case, it will simply be information and knowledge that becomes a part of your Acquired Self.

After a while, my patient was able to be free of anxiety and insomnia and did not need any anti-anxiety drug any longer.

Fear of Disease, Disability and Death

Fear of disease comes from fear of losing health. For example, you read in an article how someone developed cancer (lost his health) and died after a painful period of being in and out of the hospital. You store this virtual experience along with its sad emotions in your memory box. Next time you hear the word cancer it may trigger thoughts like "what if it happens to me" and the mind creates a long virtual movie of your potential painful experience. You may become so fearful that you end up losing sleep.

Fear itself is detrimental to your health and plays a significant role in the development of any disease including cancer. What an irony!

Most people are fearful of dying. Others may say that they are not afraid of dying, but they don't want any pain or suffering due to a disease or disability. They would rather die peacefully in their sleep. They don't want to be in a wheelchair due to a stroke or be in chronic pain, say due to a back injury.

Many people simply hate the idea of death and want to beat it at all costs.

The Root Cause Of Fear Of Disease, Disability and Death

Have you ever wondered who it is in you who is afraid of disease, disability and death? It's your Acquired Self, isn't it?

Your Acquired Self, being virtual in nature, is in constant fear of dying. It comes up with a variety of reasons why it shouldn't die. For example, it may say that it does not want to leave any loved ones behind, especially its children, although they may be grown-ups and have their own children. It wants to live forever for one reason or another. It hates any change. It wants the *status quo* to continue. That's why it wants its health to continue forever. It wants to stay in control and does not want to be vulnerable. It especially does not want to be dependent on others. That's why it is afraid of disability.

However, everything keeps changing. *That is the law of the universe.* Health certainly keeps changing. One day you're healthy, the next day you're sick. One day you're totally independent, the next day, you're disabled and totally dependent on others.

Death is the ultimate reality we all face one day. However, to the Acquired Self, the idea of death is a threat to its own existence. That's why it hates death. Any reminder about the ultimate reality of death triggers a potential threat to its existence and this perceived threat produces fear. That's why your Acquired Self fights disease (instead of working with the body to take care of it), hoping to avoid death forever.

Death is perceived as something bad, terrible and therefore, highly undesirable. The Collective Acquired Self of society negatively feeds your individual Acquired Self around the word "DEATH."

For example, the most severe penalty for a crime is the death penalty. You often read in the newspaper: the wrongful death, the death toll, the premature death, the unexpected death, cheating death, the jaws of death.

Your Acquired Self has been programmed to stay in control to be secure. However, it also keeps being reminded that it can't stay in control forever. This sense of inability to control creates fear which then can lead to symptoms of anxiety and panic attack.

Freedom From The Fear Of Disease, Disability and Death

As most people are in the grip of their Acquired Self, many are also in the grip of fear of disease, disability and death.

If you use logic, you realize that birth and death are tied together; two sides of one coin. If you are born, you are going to die. This is the law of nature.

Once you clearly see this law of birth and death, you can be free of your conditioned mind, who wants to stay in denial of this very basic fact.

Pondering over death can be very liberating. Realizing that every day is bringing you closer to the "day of your exit" will wake you up from psychological sleep. Then, you start to live every day to its fullest.

Even death is no more than passing away to another dimension. There doesn't have to be anything scary about it.

Please read more on this topic in my book, "Wake Up While You Can"

Once free of the concept of living a disease-free life forever, you start to experience life. Instead of wasting all your energy trying to defy disease and death, and live in fear, you realize that at this very moment, you are alive. Get rid of fear and start living every moment with joy, peace, and pleasure.

Phobias

Phobias are another manifestation of fear. Your Acquired Self often thinks like this: "I must never face this kind of dangerous situation again. What can I do to prevent it from happening?"

For example, if you had a bad experience in the wilderness, your Acquired Self may say, "I should avoid going into the wild." This type of thinking leads to "avoidance behavior."

Sometimes, it may not even be your own experience. If you hear or read about traumatic experiences of others at airports or during flights, then your Acquired Self may decide *not* to take trips on airplanes anymore.

As a child, if you hear from your parents that someone died from a bee sting, you may become fearful of bees and avoid going to the park that you previously used to love to visit. Even worse, if you happen to be stung by a bee and your parents create a huge drama (even though nothing serious happened to you), you will likely develop a phobia for insects.

Now don't take me wrong. Your parents take all these measures out of their love for you, so nothing bad should ever happen to you. Just the thought of what could have happened to you because of a bee sting creates a lot of anxiety for your parents.

Often these traumatic, threatening experiences get pushed into the subconscious or even unconscious part of your mind. On the surface, everything is fine, but you want to stay in total control.

Certain situations where you don't have full control, such as in a crowd, an elevator or an airplane, can give rise to intense anxiety and even a panic attack. Then, you start to avoid crowds (which is called agoraphobia) or avoid closed spaces (which is called claustrophobia).

There are many other forms of phobias such as fear of germs, spiders, height, darkness, thunder and lightning, needles, water, public speaking, etc.

Freedom From Phobias

Clearly see that the root cause of your phobia is your own Acquired Self. Obviously, freedom from the Acquired Self means freedom from phobias. But how to do it? Here are practical steps to become free of phobias:

Stop running away (avoidance behavior), because it strengthens the grip of the phobia. When you avoid certain so-called threatening factors or situations, you are telling your brain that a thing or a situation is going to be bad, threatening, painful, etc. "Therefore, I am avoiding it."

Your brain listens to your command and makes sure you stay away from the so-called threatening factor or situation. Therefore, it will trigger a huge release of adrenaline as you are about to encounter the so-called threatening factor or situation, which will trigger anxiety (or even a panic attack). Obviously, you will run away from the situation, which will further strengthen the grip of your phobias on you.

Instead, use the Mind-Body connection to your advantage. Tell your brain with conviction that you are *not* afraid of closed spaces, crowds, height, insects, germs, needles, water, heights, darkness, or whatever it may be.

Imagine that you are in the situation (closed space, height, crowds, blood draw station) or picture an insect, germ, water, etc. -or whatever you are afraid of. *Tell your brain it is not frightening.* You are not afraid of what you are seeing in your imagination. Initially, you may feel an adrenaline rush and that is okay. Practice it repeatedly till you get to the point that there is no adrenaline rush.

Now you are ready to face real situations such as closed space, crowds, height, blood draw facility, or a factor such as an insect, germ, or water.

Some people can use their Mind-Body connection with conviction during a so-called threatening situation such as being in a crowd, closed space, or a blood draw facility. Once they ride the adrenaline rush without running away from the situation, they get over their phobia right away.

Remember anxiety never kills anyone. You are part of the Divine. Therefore, you are indestructible.

Fear Can Express As Anger And Hate

Sometimes fear can express as anger and hate.

For example, let's say you had a bad experience, and your conditioned mind doesn't want it to ever happen again. Therefore, it wants to stay in total control all the time. Even the thought of losing control creates a huge amount of fear.

It may go an extra step to pursue security for itself and its loved ones. For instance, like in the earlier example of encountering a bear, you may start to think, "Maybe I should also protect other humans from this dangerous creature called a bear. I should join a group that kills bears and similar beasts that endanger my fellow human beings.

In addition to fear, now you have also developed *hate* towards wild beasts. You may express this hate verbally, in writing or even physically. This is how deep-seated fear expresses itself as anger, rage, and hate.

Now imagine you meet a person or a group who, due to their own Acquired Self, loves wild beasts and wants to protect them by spending taxpayer's money (that includes you!). You start hating these kinds of people and groups. You may even join a group or a party that collectively hates wild beasts and wild-beast lovers. Now you have a mission in life. Each time you listen to a radio program (or podcast) in which so-called experts talk about saving wild beasts, your blood starts boiling. You may even call the radio station and express your point of view. You may even be invited to one of these shows. Now you can tell your story and fight the other expert, who tells his story and opposes your point of view. Both of you may get into heated arguments.

Learn how to be free of anger in the next chapter.

Summary Of Harmful Effects Of Fear

In summary, fear is the underlying cause of symptoms of uneasiness, jitteriness, restlessness, insomnia, anxiety, panic attacks, phobias, hate, anger, arguments, and physical or verbal violence. In addition, it causes high blood pressure, high blood sugar, acute heart attacks, pounding of heart, chest tightness or pain, air hunger, feeling of passing out, migraine headaches, irritable bowel syndrome, dementia, and a long list of autoimmune diseases.

Fear Can Be Addictive

An adrenaline rush also gives you a feeling of excitement, but then this feeling goes away. Of course, you want more excitement. So, you look for fear. Plenty of it is available in the form of sensational news in the media. You also get it by repeatedly talking to yourself or someone else about your bad experiences.

In your social encounters, you love to talk about sensational, fearful stories. Other people readily jump in and validate your stories with their own stories. Soon you and your friends will be sitting in a cloud of fear and loving it.

Next time, watch how people talk at workplaces or at parties and notice how everyone joins in as soon as someone tells a fearful story. Everyone loves to outdo others by telling more intense fearful stories.

Sometimes, you decide to watch a scary movie to feed your appetite for fear. Many people become addicted to fear.

Fear Sells

In the grip of fear, you can't think with logic. You simply want security at any cost. The Collective Acquired Self knows it very well. So first it creates fear for you and then it can sell you whatever it wants, in the name of providing security. In this way, fear is very profitable and generates big business. These days the whole world makes use of this strategy of creating fear and selling whatever they want.

Freedom From Fear

Once you realize that fear is a product of your own conditioned mind – the Acquired Self – you can be free of its tight grip by dissociating from your Acquired Self. Simply utilize your Acquired Self to function in society, but don't get enslaved by it.

Being fearless does not mean you become reckless and oblivious to obvious dangers. Be prudent, but not over-cautious. Be practical.

For example, if someone in your family or at work has some contagious illness such as Flu or Covid, take sensible precautions to keep some distance, wash your hands frequently and boost up your immune system by taking Zinc, Vitamin D3, chewing on cloves and sipping Ginger and honey tea.

Don't go to extremes such as not taking any precautions or the other extreme of fleeing your house or workplace altogether.

CHAPTER: 14

AN ANGRY WORLD

The Human World is filled with angry people. Most people think it is part of living and there is no way around it. Many even justify their anger, especially if they are part of a "collective anger of a group." Many cultural, political and religious groups harbor collective anger.

Stressful World Of Anger

When you are angry, you create huge stress for yourself and everyone else around you. In the heat of anger, you may spew out a flurry of insulting, hateful remarks which can provoke others. They get angry and return even stronger hateful and insulting remarks to you. If the drama of verbal violence continues, it can lead to physical violence.

A World Of Frustrations, Irritations, And Annoyances

In a less dramatic version, anger takes the form of annoyances, irritations and frustrations. Often, you keep it to yourself. This creates a constant sense of irritability and tension inside you. Sometimes, you verbalize your frustrations in a "civilized" manner.

Often, others don't seem to care or may even disagree with your point of view, which upsets you even more. You may promise yourself you're not going to get into any arguments to keep peace. In this way, you suppress your anger to be civil and polite. However, you feel annoyed and irritated inside… and little things make you more irritated and annoyed.

In some cases, suppression of frustration and anger, especially from childhood, gets so deep that you have no clue where your "comfort eating" comes from. Many people get depressed.

Harmful Effects Of Anger

Anger causes excess release of adrenaline (and noradrenaline) from our adrenal glands. High adrenaline level wreaks havoc on our health and puts us at risk of high blood pressure, heart attack, stroke, Type 2 diabetes, dementia, and cancer – just to name a few.

In addition, anger tarnishes our mental and spiritual health tremendously.

The Root Cause Of Anger

Use logic and examine what underlies your anger. In most individuals, anger is a product of one or several components of your Acquired Self, the Monster within.

1. Expectations

One of the basic reasons for frustration and anger is your expectations. You had certain expectations which did not come through and that's why you feel disappointed, frustrated and angry.

What Is The Basis Of Expectations?

Use logic and you will find that expectations really are a collection of concepts you acquire during your upbringing. These become part of your Acquired Self. These concepts revolve around how others should behave towards you and how you should behave towards them. For example, you expect certain kinds of behavior from your spouse, parents, brothers, sisters, friends and colleagues and vice versa. In a way, society dictates how each of us should fulfill our role. We can call it the "book of role descriptions," written by the Collective Acquired Self of Society. Every person living in a particular society is downloaded with its book of role descriptions.

Everyone knows the description of his/her role and knows the description of the others' role. For example, this book tells you how a wife should behave, how a husband should behave, how a parent should behave, how a friend should behave, how a child should behave, how a teacher should behave, how a doctor should behave, etc. Automatically it gives rise to certain expectations.

You expect others to play their part right, by the book. They expect you to play your role right. In other words, everyone is judging everyone else.

Now what happens if someone doesn't play their part right? You get frustrated and at times angry. Actually, it's your Acquired Self who feels let down, frustrated and angry, because it is the Acquired Self who builds up expectations. Your Acquired Self believes in the concepts contained in the book of role descriptions. The more you believe in the book of role descriptions, the more likely you suffer from anger.

The closer the relationship, the higher the expectations… and more emotional pain if someone does not meet your expectations. This emotional pain manifests as annoyances, frustrations and anger.

Examples:

- A spouse falling off the ladder of expectations is the most frequent cause of divorce. It goes something like this: In a marriage, as soon as the period of intense sexual romance has cooled, the two monsters (Acquired Selves) show their true faces. Now each spouse starts seeing faults in the other person as the person is not living up to expectations. This initially causes annoyance which continues to build up in their memory box and eventually leads to pain and anger. Then one day, there is a big blow up and the marriage ends up in a divorce. Your Monster of expectations is very judgmental and always finds faults in others. Interestingly, it does not see any faults with itself.

- Brothers, sisters and close friends get mad and angry if their expectations are not met. Sometimes they end up losing lifelong relationships.
- Kids failing to meet the expectations of their parents cause a lot of pain and suffering for their parents as well as themselves. For example, Dad expected his son to become a doctor, but his son got poor grades in school. This caused severe headaches and ugly arguments between Dad and his son.
- Mom expected her daughter to marry someone of the same religious faith, but her daughter married someone of a different religion. Another cause of anger and pain.
- A wife expected a gift on her birthday but didn't get anything. The result? Hurt, pain, and anger.
- A husband expected his wife to be nice to his rowdy

buddies, but she called them immature dirt bags which caused a huge argument, pain, and anger.

- An employee expected a promotion, but didn't get it which caused pain and resentment.
- A person expected wonderful golden years after retirement but developed cancer which resulted in bitterness and anger.
- A patient expected a high level of care from his doctor. However, he found out his doctor provided poor care. The result? A lot of anger and often a reason for a lawsuit if you live in the U.S.A.
- In addition to their own personal life, people also build expectations around political and religious figures, movie stars, singers, artists, etc. and get very disappointed and angry if their icon doesn't live up to their expectations. Some even get so angry that they end up killing their icon.
- People also create expectations around political, economic, and religious systems and get very upset once their expectations are not fulfilled.

- People even have expectations about "how long they will live." It is called "life expectancy." Hence, they feel cheated if someone close to them dies before they are supposed to.
- The Human World promises that you will be rewarded if

you follow the rules and punished if you don't. Now what happens if you follow the rules and don't get rewarded and someone who doesn't follow the rules gets rewarded? You get very upset and angry. For example, you are an honest person suffering economic hardships while some crooked, dishonest, liar is rolling in money. "Life isn't fair" you may find yourself saying. You feel very disappointed and angry at life.

True Freedom from Expectations

To be free of anger, you need to be free of expectations. Realize your True Self has no expectations whatsoever! It's the Acquired Self who builds up all the expectations and gets hurt when these expectations are not met.

With this realization, you can be free of expectations because they are not part of who you truly are. You can simply let go of the parasite that is eating you up. Once you get rid of the root cause, then frustration, annoyance, and anger simply do not arise. Then you don't have to practice certain techniques to manage your anger.

2. Self-righteousness

Another common reason for anger and frustration is self-righteousness.

What is self-righteousness? In simple terms, it means "I am right." It also implies that "you are wrong." This is the root cause of all disagreements, disputes, arguments, quarrels, fights, lawsuits, battles, and wars.

With few exceptions, everyone suffers from self-righteousness. Interestingly, people don't like to be called self-righteous because it's considered a bad quality. They don't think they are self-righteous, but they readily see it in others. They simply judge others to be self-righteous and don't go any deeper. They believe they are correct that someone else is self-righteous. Interesting, isn't it?

Self-righteousness is an extremely common affliction and one of the major reasons for all human conflicts. If we want to understand human conflicts, it makes sense to look at self-righteousness more deeply.

What Is The Basis Of Self-Righteousness?

We interpret people, objects, and events through the filters of stored information, knowledge, concepts, ideas, stories of our own experiences, others' experiences, and collective human experiences, etc. Basically, it consists of tons of information (and associated emotions) which we acquire as we grow up.

Obviously, this stored information varies from person to person. Therefore, interpretation of the same event, person, and object varies from person to person. When you completely identify with your Acquired Self, you strongly believe that your interpretation is right, which of course is self-righteousness.

In addition, the book of role descriptions is an important part of the Acquired Self. This book (as we observed earlier) describes how a person should and should not behave in a given society. In addition to creating expectations, it also provides a background against which everyone keeps judging others behavior. It tells you and everyone else "what is right and what is wrong," "what is virtue and what is evil." This is the basis of morality.

These are basically concepts given to you by your Society's Collective Acquired Self. Now, if you are in the total grip of your Acquired Self, you believe these concepts to be the truth. You honestly believe that you are right, because you follow the concepts of morality, which of course is self-righteousness. In addition, you believe those who don't follow these concepts are wrong.

In addition to the book of role descriptions, your Society's Collective Acquired Self also downloads many other concepts into your Acquired Self. For example, it gives you the concepts about "your rights," "human rights," and "animal rights." All these concepts become part of your Acquired Self and give you more ammunition to be right. In this way, these concepts strengthen your self-righteousness.

Furthermore, your Society's Collective Acquired Self downloads the knowledge of history into your Acquired Self, which primarily is an interpretation of certain events by the Acquired Self of the historian. That is why there are so many different interpretations of the same event and of course, every historian believes he is right.

The historian's interpretation of events becomes part of your Acquired Self, and you believe them to be true although the event may have happened before you (and the historian) were even born. Different Acquired Selves with different versions of the same historic event or historic figure then get into heated arguments and get angry at each other.

With background knowledge of history, your Acquired Self also judges current political events. Usually, it is some so-called expert who does it for you on a TV show, in a newspaper, or in a book.

Acquired Selves with different versions of history interpret current events differently and each one believes he is right. Consequently, people get into heated arguments and get angry at each other.

It is interesting to note that in a society, there are collective concepts about what is right and what is wrong. This creates a collective self-righteousness, which gets reinforced constantly by the news media in that society. What is right in one society may be wrong in another society. This creates conflict between various societies. That's why people living in one society get angry at another society. This is the basis of collective conflict, anger, and violence between various nations.

Then, within a given society, there are various concepts about what is right and what is wrong, depending upon various social, political, and religious groups in that society. This creates conflict, anger, and violence between various groups within society.

Within a group, there are various concepts about what is right and what is wrong. Therefore, within the same group, people get angry and fight among each other. Even within a family, there are various concepts about what is right and what is wrong. It leads to conflict, anger, and violence (usually verbal but sometimes even physical) between various members of the same family. For example, you may believe in one political candidate and your husband in an opposing candidate. This could lead to serious arguments, verbal conflict, and tons of anger.

Within an individual, there are conflicting concepts of what is right and what is wrong. There is one code of ethics for the workplace and another one for home, one code of ethics for friends and another one for enemies, one standard for yourself and another one for everyone else. It all boils down to "I, My, Me" which is the core of the Acquired Self.

True Freedom from Self-Righteousness

If you want to be free of self-righteousness, you need to

first admit that you are suffering from self-righteousness. And here is the biggest dilemma - when you strongly believe that you are right, how can you ever admit that you are not right? That's why most people continue to suffer from self-righteousness and its consequences of anger and even hate.

If you are willing to entertain the idea that you may not be right, then there is a chance that you may get freedom from the prison of self-righteousness.

Once you have a logical insight into the mechanics of self-righteousness, you will happily get out of the prison of self-righteousness. With that, anger automatically dies out.

3. Control the Behavior of Others

We all want to control the behavior of others. That's why we get very upset if we are unable to control others.

Why do you want to control someone's behavior? Because your Acquired Self is full of expectations. When you have certain expectations, you are automatically trying to control someone's behavior, *albeit* in a passive way.

For example, you expect your husband to be faithful to you and should never have sex with anyone else. In a passive way, you are trying to control your husband's behavior. Obviously, you will get angry if you are unable to control his behavior.

In addition, the Acquired Self is inherently insecure. It

feels safe if it can control the behavior of others.

It is interesting to note that no one wants to be controlled, but everyone wants to control others.

Freedom From Urge To Control

As we observed earlier, expectations arise out of society's "Book of Role Descriptions." If you believe in it, you will continue to have the urge to control the behavior of others, and the drama of irritation, frustration, and anger will continue.

Use logic and realize everyone is a human being, born free, and does not need to be on a leash. Then, you can use society's "Book Of Role Descriptions" to function in the world, but don't believe it to be some kind of ultimate truth.

For example, you may decide to get married and raise children according to the "Book Of Role Descriptions" in your part of the world. However, it does not mean that you now suddenly own your spouse and put them on a leash.

Once you are free of the tight grip of your Acquired Self, you get in touch with your True Self which is free, joyful, content and has no insecurity. Thereafter, the urge to control automatically dies out.

4. Fear

Another reason why people get angry is their deep-seated fear, but they usually don't know it. The more short-tempered a person is on the surface, the more fearful they are inside.

Expressing anger outwardly is a gesture of extreme insecurity inside. People try to scare others with their anger, while they themselves are fearful. How ironic!

Most people don't even realize that their "bursts of anger" arise out of a volcano of fear and insecurity.

The Root Cause of Fear

Fear arises from the memory of a bad event, which tells you to learn from your past.

How your Acquired Self learns from it's past may go something like this: "This must never happen again!" Then comes another thought - "what if" - and that creates a huge amount of fear. In this way, your Acquired Self becomes quite insecure. Hence, it seeks security. In the pursuit of security, it wants to control the behavior of others. However, when it can't control others, it gets very angry. Even a trigger in the form of a comment, news article or a story that reminds the Acquired Self it cannot control others, can throw it into a rage.

True Freedom from Fear

You can be free of fear once and for all only when you know the root cause of fear. Then, there is no need to learn various techniques to control your fear.

As we observed, fear arises from some bad memories in the past and the mind's attempt to prevent similar bad things from happening again. You must realize that the "bad event" is not happening at this moment. It happened, yes, but it is not happening at this moment. It is being kept alive only through the activity of your own mind. Otherwise, it is dead and gone. This realization will free you from fear.

Because the memory of a bad event does not control your mind anymore, there is no need to think this may happen again and obviously, your mind does not create more thoughts on how to prevent it. That's how the whole infrastructure of anger simply crumbles and you get the ultimate freedom from fear and anger.

5. Insults

Another reason why people get angry is insults. Many people fight back by returning insulting remarks or gestures. However, some pretend to be polite and civilized on the surface, while fuming with anger underneath. Later, they often express their anger while talking to a sympathetic ear such as their spouse, friend, or therapist.

Some even suppress anger so deeply that on the surface, they manage to remain polite and civilized all the time. They may even try to fake a smile, but deep inside, they feel irritated and don't even know why they feel that way!

What is the Basis of Insults?

To be truly free of insults, you first need to figure out

who it is inside you who gets insulted in the first place.

Use logic and you will find that it's your Acquired Self who gets insulted. The True Self never gets insulted. Why do I say that? Because a newborn baby never gets insulted. You can try to insult a baby by saying whatever you want, but the baby will not be insulted.

In the same way, imagine someone trying to insult you in a language that you don't understand. Obviously, you will not be insulted. Therefore, we can conclude that for the insult to occur, you need to understand the concepts attached to those words and gestures. Otherwise, they have no power.

Where do you learn the words and gestures and all concepts attached to them? You are not born with them. You obviously learn them as you grow up in the Human World. That's why it is logical to conclude it's your Acquired Self who gets insulted.

With every word, there is a concept attached. For example, the word STUPID has a whole concept of unintelligence, inadequacy and worthlessness attached to it. When your developing Acquired Self learns this word, it stores all the negative concepts attached to the word. If someone calls you that word, the negative concept attached to that word is activated. Then, the negative thought that I am unintelligent, inadequate and worthless triggers negative emotions. You feel unintelligent, inadequate, and worthless. You didn't deserve it.

How dare someone say that to you. Your Acquired Self's sense of self-esteem is threatened. Therefore, it fights back verbally or even physically to secure its existence, its self-esteem.

The insulting words are created by Society's Collective Acquired Self for individual Acquired Selves to fight with each other, aren't they?

Society's Collective Acquired Self downloads the concept of "insult and respect" into your Acquired Self. When others respect you, your Acquired Self feels validated and when others insult you, your Acquired Self feels humiliated. In other words, your Acquired Self is constantly reacting to how others treat it. Your Acquired Self wants to be respected and not be insulted. Obviously, it has no control over others' behavior, but it doesn't know this basic fact. It just keeps searching for respect and running away from insult. It is especially true if at an early age you were insulted (teased) a lot. Your Acquired Self felt humiliated and all those painful experiences become part of your Acquired Self.

Then, your Acquired Self found a way to excel (academics, money, sports, etc.) and became successful, accomplished, and wealthy. Obviously, it starts to *expect* respect from others, especially those who once insulted him. The more it gets attached to respect, the more it resents the idea of insult. Then, a trivial teasing remark can upset your Acquired Self for days. You may even burst into anger in a social situation where you didn't get enough respect, which you perceive as an insult.

True Freedom From Insults

Often, others (usually those who care about you) can see your over-reactions and suggest anger management. So, you try the usual venues society offers such as counseling, books, seminars, etc., but nothing really works for you. Sooner or later, you again explode in a rage, or you sizzle inside over some insulting remark someone made months or even years ago. Many people stay trapped in the prison of insults for the rest of their life.

Is it possible to be free of insults? The answer is yes, but only when you get to the root of the problem. When you realize that it is really your Acquired Self that gets insulted, you can free yourself from your Acquired Self.

Then, you realize that it is your Acquired Self who is holding onto painful memories when it felt insulted. Use common sense and realize those painful experiences are not happening in the present moment. They are only happening in your head. This simple realization can free you of the huge load of painful memories.

You also realize that you don't have to keep proving your worth and chasing praise from others. In this way, the need for praise simply vanishes. Then, you don't react to remarks of praise or insult. People can say whatever they want: it does not make you elated or angry.

Free of your Acquired Self, you live in joy, peace, and bliss that is never threatened.

Once you fully realize the mechanics of insulting words, you'll laugh (in your head) when someone uses an insulting remark, won't you? Because you will see that the other person's Acquired Self is doing what it has been conditioned to do and it does not mean a thing. Then, there is no need to fight back.

It is quite likely that even with all this wisdom, your Acquired Self will get engaged and fight back next time you're insulted. However, minutes or even hours later, you may be able to see the "real mechanics of insult."

The moment you see insult in its true colors, you'll be free of it, instead of fuming for days. In this way, no one will be able to insult you. People may try to insult you, but you won't get insulted.

Q: *I can't accept the fact that there are so many bad people in the world. How can I not be angry?*

A: Instead of being angry, isn't it worthwhile examining why people act in a bad way?

If you use logic, then you will find that the root cause of all bad behavior is in fact, the individual Acquired Self, as well as Society's Collective Acquired Self. The most common underlying causes of bad behavior are anger and fear, arising out of expectations, self-righteousness, urge to control, insults, jealousy, greed, ego, and selfishness.

All these personality traits are ingredients of the Acquired Self. Therefore, the Human World cannot be free of bad behavior so long as it is in the grip of Society's Collective Acquired Self.

When you are in the grip of the Acquired Self, you see faults with everyone except yourself. The fact is that everyone who is in the grip of the Acquired Self ends up with so-called bad behavior, whether he admits it or not.

CHAPTER: 15

A HATEFUL WORLD

Hate and Grievances are very deep-seated emotions. Revenge is an action arising out of grievances and hate. Not only do individuals harbor hate, but groups of people, societies, and nations also harbor hate and grievances.

Harmful Effects Of Hate, Grievances And Revenge

While hate creates constant burning and irritation inside you, revenge arising out of this hate inflicts tremendous suffering on other human beings. However, you don't look on them as human beings. ***The fire of hate makes you totally blind.***

You look at others as your enemies – not human beings – who must be defeated, destroyed, and annihilated. Your actions obviously reinforce hate in others, who try to inflict suffering on you as much as they can and the "ping - pong of violence" continues.

Deep down, you and your enemies are also afraid of each other. The desire to dominate and annihilate each other becomes increasingly intense. Therefore, you and your enemies are constantly at work developing new tricks, new strategies, new technologies, and new weapons to dominate, defeat, and annihilate each other. This is the basis of the never-ending cycle of wars.

Harmful Effects Of Hate On Health

In addition to creating suffering for humanity, hate harms our physical, mental, and spiritual health.

When we are hateful, our body produces excessive amounts of adrenaline (and noradrenaline) and cortisol, whether we are winning or losing in a conflict.

High adrenaline (noradrenaline) and cortisol levels wreak havoc on our health and puts us at risk of high blood pressure, heart attack, stroke, weight gain, Type 2 diabetes, dementia, and cancer – just to name a few.

Moreover, hate damages our mental health, and tarnishes our spiritual health to an unimaginable degree.

Superficial Solution Of Hate

Sooner or later, you get tired of the huge stress that hate and grievances create for you and others. You want to find some answers, so you turn to your Society's Collective

Acquired Self. What does it tell you? "Hate, grievances and revenge are not good. You should be loving and peaceful. You should be non-violent."

That sounds wonderful, but in the next breath it also advises you "to fight and defeat your enemies." In essence, what Society's Collective Acquired Self tells you is to pick and choose. "Be peaceful and loving towards your friends but be hateful and vengeful towards your enemies."

Well, as we all know, this philosophy does not work at all. That's why there's so much hate, revenge, and violence inside you, all around you, and in the world despite all sorts of religious, social, and political preaching promoting non-violence, peace, and love.

Is It Possible To Be Free Of Hate, Grievances And Revenge?

Is it possible to be rid of hate, grievances and revenge? Society's Collective Acquired Self will tell you that it is not possible. It may even tell you that hate is part of "human nature." "You fight for your survival. Therefore, fighting is human nature."

This type of explanation becomes part of your Acquired Self, which therefore justifies hate and violence.

Is it possible for you to be free of hate and revenge? If you earnestly try to find the answer for yourself, you need to set aside all explanations you have been given. Only then can you look at the problem with logic. Like a true scientist, you must be free of all preconceived notions to investigate a problem.

What Is The Root Cause Of Hate And Grievances?

To cure hate, you need to diagnose its root cause, right? What is the root cause of hate and grievances? Why do you hate someone? Isn't it because you believe someone is your enemy? Why do you believe that someone is your enemy? Because someone did something bad to you in the past or you've been told that someone or some group did something bad to your ancestors in the past.

"My" (or Our) enemy and "My" (or Our) past are clearly the root cause of hate and grievances.

"My" Enemy

Let's take a closer look at "My" enemy." Who is talking? It's your Acquired Self, isn't it? "I, My, Me, Mine" Syndrome, as we observed earlier, is at the core of your Acquired Self. It divides you from everyone else on the planet. Then, you perceive yourself as "I" and everyone else as "others."

You look at the world through the window of the concepts drilled into your Acquired Self such as religious, social, and political ideas. Those who have similar ideas to your Acquired Self become your friends. On the other hand, those with opposing ideas become your enemies. This is the basis of "My" (or Our) enemies.

"My" Past

Now let's look at "My" (or Our) past. What is the past? Your Acquired Self takes a mental picture of every event and judges it good or bad based upon the "book of role descriptions" already downloaded in it. Judging triggers an emotion and then, the whole bundle of "event, judgment, and emotion" get stored in memory. That's how your mind creates your past. Later, it visits the stored events (memories) over and over again.

Let's say, you had an event that your Acquired Self judged to be a defeat due to unfairness and stored it as a bad memory. Each time your mind visits this unfair event of defeat, you feel a wave of rage rising inside you.

Unfairness triggers bitterness, hate, and rage. Now, you want to defeat the person who defeated you in the past and caused you so much stress. You want to get even and cause him pain and suffering. Only this time around, you may use any means. You will even be unfair. "So what? I was a victim of unfairness once," you rationalize. Society's Collective

Acquired Self validates these thoughts. "There is no fairness in war. Life is unfair."

In the grip of your hate and grievances, you (and collectively, your group) become so irrational that you may inflict pain and suffering on people who have nothing to do with your past. It is usually people with less power, such as your employees, children, women, and underprivileged people. You just want to "give it to someone."

Fire Of History

In addition to your personal past, Society's Collective Acquired Self has created its own collective past called history, which is downloaded into your Acquired Self as part of your upbringing. This is the basis of collective grievances and bitterness against a certain historic figure or a group of people.

Perpetuation of bitterness and grievances often leads to violence which creates more bad memories and feeds more bitterness and grievances. That's how hate thrives.

True Freedom From Hate, Grievances And Revenge

Now for a moment consider that you are free of "I, My, Me, Mine" Syndrome and free of the personal as well as the collective past. Do you have any hate or grievances left? The answer obviously is No! When you are free of hate and grievance, you are automatically free of the desire to avenge.

Now the big question is how do you get freedom from the "I, My, Me, Mine" Syndrome? Use logic and you realize you were not born with this. It was given to you by your Collective Acquired Self.

How do you get freedom from your personal and collective past? Use logic and realize that the past only exists in your head. Of course, it was real when it happened, but now it is a phantom - unreal because it is not happening in the Now.

Once free of the "I, My, Me, Mine" Syndrome and free of the past, you will not have any hate or grievances. Then obviously, you won't have any enemies. Automatically, there is no need to take revenge. That's how violence ends spontaneously.

Q: Aren't hate and violence human nature?

A: Hate and violence are the nature of the Acquired Self. If you totally identify with your Acquired Self and that's who you think you are, then you will believe that hate and violence are human nature.

Society's Collective Acquired Self reinforces this concept into your Acquired Self. "Everyone else believes in it.

I saw experts on TV believing in it, so it must be true," says your Acquired Self.

Only when you are free of your Acquired Self, can you clearly see that hate, grievance, and violence are the product of the Acquired Self.

If you want to see true human nature, observe newborn babies. They are not hateful or violent, are they? On the contrary, they are so peaceful, loving, and joyful. They don't judge anyone because of color, creed, religion, or nationality. They have no enemies. They don't hold hate or grievances because they are devoid of the "Acquired Self."

Q: *I hate violence. I believe in non-violence, peace, and love. I have joined groups who promote these wonderful ideas. Isn't that great?*

A: Violence is the result of hate. When you say," I hate violence," aren't you adding fuel to the fire? Don't you have to look at hate itself? What's the root cause of hate? Once you figure that out, then you can be free of violence without hating violence.

As we observed earlier, hate is the product of the Acquired Self. Certain ideas such as non-violence and world peace seem noble and wonderful. However, any idea or concept is ultimately part of the Acquired Self.

As long as people are in the grip of their Acquired Selves, they are divided from each other. While there is division, there will be conflict. It is so logical!

Conflict is the foundation of violence and peace cannot be when there is violence. Therefore, peace cannot be while people are in the grip of their Acquired Selves.

Concepts divide human beings into groups. This is the basis of conflict and violence. Any concept, however wonderful and noble, cannot (and obviously has not) free humans from conflict and violence.

Q: Isn't "survival of the fittest" the basis of our evolution? Therefore, shouldn't we be strong in order to survive?

A: What Darwin proposed as the basis of evolution was "the process of natural selection," which later, the laymen press changed into "survival of the fittest." In fact, survival of the most *adaptable* is a more accurate interpretation of "the process of natural selection." Fittest is not the most accurate interpretation, because it somehow points towards being powerful. As we know, some of the most powerful animals, such as dinosaurs, are extinct now and some of the weakest animals, such as ants and butterflies, have survived the hardships of nature.

When we talk about survival in terms of evolution, we talk of the real survival of a species. When people talk of survival of the fittest, they give it as an excuse for wars and killing other human beings. Obviously, they are not talking about the survival of the collective human race. They are talking of survival of those humans who have similar ideas and concepts as their own. They are talking about survival of their own Collective Acquired Selves, aren't they?

Q: Violence is part of nature. You see it when an animal kills another animal. So why are people so against violence these days?

A: You are confusing killing with violence. To you, killing means violence. In nature, when an animal kills another animal, it is either hungry, defending itself, or protecting its babies from predators. However, when people kill each other, they usually don't do it because they are hungry or threatened.

Humans often kill each other because they are psychologically threatened, although there is often no real threat to their existence as humans. They wage wars to defend their religious, nationalistic, or political ideologies. They often kill others, not because they are hungry, but to have more land, more wealth, more power, etc.

Now when an animal kills another animal, it is not defending its religious or political beliefs. However, looking through the filters of your Acquired Self, you call it violence and therefore, justify the violence that people carry out against each other.

The Acquired Self is very cunning, clever and treacherous. It lures you with very noble, wonderful, and intellectually appealing ideas. However, you can cut through its disguise with logic, your ultimate intelligence.

Q: *I am trying hard to be non-violent, peaceful and loving. Can you suggest some techniques?*

A: Violence and hate are the products of the Acquired Self. In contrast, your True Self, the one you are born with, is non-violent, loving, and peaceful. This is your true nature and that is the true nature of every other human being as well.

As you can see, you already have this wonderful human being sitting inside you. The source of love, peace, and nonviolence is inside you - your True Self, but it gets eclipsed by your Acquired Self.

Lost in the Acquired Self, you search for something out there which already resides inside you. You search for concepts and ideas to be non-violent, peaceful, and loving. All concepts are part of the Acquired Self. Therefore, the more you search for nonviolence, peace, and love, the more you get in the grip of your Acquired Self and the farther you get from your True Self. Can you understand how counterproductive your search for nonviolence, love, and peace is?

So, stop searching for nonviolence, love, and peace. All you need to do is be free of your Acquired Self and let your True Self illuminate you. The True Self is real, not a concept. Therefore, you can only experience it, feel it, be it. You cannot describe it. Why? Because words themselves are products of Society's Collective Acquired Self. Words create concepts and the True Self is not a concept.

Q: I see so much violence and suffering in the world. I want to change the world. I believe love can change the world. That is my mission: to change the world with love.

A: People have been trying to change the world with a variety of wonderful ideas including the idea of love. However, the reality is something like this: Over the last 5000 years or so of known human history, people have not changed a bit, in psychological terms. We have made great progress in terms of technology, but psychologically speaking, we humans are as violent, hateful, revengeful, jealous, and fearful as we ever were. Why?

Before you answer, please be still for a moment. Take a fresh look at the root cause of violence and suffering before you embark on the mission to cure this widespread ailment of human beings.

As we observed earlier, the root cause of violence is conflict, which results from human beings divided into groups because of concepts. In other words, attachment to concepts divides human beings from each other which leads to conflict and violence.

To put it in another way, it is the Acquired Self that separates humans from each other. As long as humans are separated from each other, there will be conflict and violence. Instead of looking at the root cause of violence and human suffering, the Acquired Self distracts you by conveniently providing you with more concepts such as love, peace, and nonviolence. By creating this distraction, the Acquired Self skillfully avoids detection and continues to thrive.

Now perhaps, you understand why humans have not changed their psychological behavior. As a byproduct of evolution and civilization, the human mind created the Acquired Self in every individual. In the grip of the Acquired Self, humans got divided and created a huge amount of suffering for each other. Then, they made sure to download their Acquired selves into their children. That's how Acquired self has thrived over thousands of years and perpetuated violence.

Everyone wants to change the world according to their own wishes and concepts. Deep down, everyone wants to control the world by changing it according to their own likes and dislikes, according to their own ideas and concepts. In doing so, they create more conflicts, more violence, and more suffering.

What is Love

Let me clarify the term Love. When we use the word love, we are talking of the concept attached to this word. The concept of love is a creation of the human mind. This love easily changes into hate when things are not the way they are supposed to be, according to the concept of love. This type of love is always conditional. You are always looking for something in return.

In contrast, there is True Love, which is not a concept and therefore cannot be described. You can feel True Love, but words do not really describe it.

CHAPTER: 16

A WORLD OF CONFLICTS

"The Human World" is a violent place since the dawn of civilization and will continue to be so until the end of civilization. Why?

Virtual Divisions

"The Human World" is divided into fragments along virtual, conceptual lines: continents, countries, cities, villages, neighborhoods, and individual homes.

However, the world is one planet without any virtual, conceptual divisions. That's why a bird can fly from one country to another without a visa or passport, but if we try to do it, we will be locked up in jail.

Us Against Them

"The Human World" is created along the lines of concepts: nationalistic, religious, financial, philosophical, racial, and cultural. These concepts divide as well as unite people. This is the basis of "Us Against Them."

For example, people in one country may get united under the umbrella of nationalism against another country. People in one religion may get united against another religion.

In addition, people living in the same country may get divided into religious, political, cultural, racial, and financial groups.

Even people in the same religious group are further divided into several subgroups of the same religion. People in the same cultural group are further divided along financial lines. People in the same financial group are further divided along political lines. There seems to be no end to the divisions in the "Human World."

In this way, concepts divide humans into groups which is the basis of "Us Against Them." Then, one group fights with another group. This is the basis of ongoing human conflicts – and violence – since the dawn of civilization and it will continue while humans stay in the grip of the Acquired Self that divides them into groups.

Harmful Effects Of Conflicts

Divisions break down universal interconnectedness, which leads to spiritual, mental, emotional, and physical suffering, not to mention immense suffering that comes from riots, battles, and wars.

In the grip of anger, hate, and revenge, our body produces excessive amounts of adrenaline (and noradrenaline) and cortisol, no matter if we are winning or losing a conflict.

High adrenaline (and noradrenaline) and cortisol levels wreak havoc on our health and puts us at risk of high blood pressure, heart attack, stroke, weight gain, Type 2 diabetes, dementia, and cancer – just to name a few.

The Concept Of Peace

When people see all the suffering inflicted by various groups onto one another, they start to wonder "What's going on?" But right there, the mastermind of the conflicts – "Society's Collective Acquired Self" – comes up with a big distraction, "World Peace."

Tolerance

"Society's Collective Acquired Self" does not address the lines of divisions that it has created. In this way, it stays under the radar. Instead, it has come up with another distraction: "The Concept of Tolerance."

"Society's Collective Acquired Self" advocates for people to cultivate tolerance, but they continue to stay in the grip of their conceptual groups along the lines of nationalism, politics, finances, religion, culture, race, philosophies, etc. Consequently, people try to tolerate those who belong to other groups and it may work for a while. However, the "fire of division" continues to smolder under the paper-thin layer of tolerance.

Sooner or later, some charismatic leader comes and fans the smoldering fire into blazing flames.

"True World Peace cannot be as long as humans stay divided due to the grip of their Acquired Selves."

Real Peace

Real peace is our true human nature. Therefore, the real solution lies within us. However, it is the Acquired Self that keeps us away from our True Self. All we have to do is to be free of the tight hold of our Acquired Self. Then, we see people as humans, not as Christians, Muslims, Hindus, etc. or Germans, Russians, Indians, etc. or socialists, communists, capitalists, etc.

Therefore, rise above the constraints of the Acquired Self. Only then do we live peacefully, and no one can shatter this peace.

CHAPTER: 17

A COMPETITIVE WORLD

Most of the "Human World" is highly competitive. We see it everywhere: at workplaces, playgrounds, schools, and even on the roads. While competition can make us better at what we do – athletes, doctors, engineers, lawyers, singers, actors – it also creates tremendous amounts of stress.

Stress Due To Competitiveness

In competitions, we either win or lose. If we win, we experience momentary thrills and excitement. On the other hand, if we lose, we feel humiliated, worthless, and even bitter if we lose due to unfairness.

Harmful Effects Of Competition On Health

The thrills and excitement of winning give us a high adrenaline rush. High adrenaline (and noradrenaline) levels wreak havoc on our physical health and puts us at risk of high blood pressure, heart attack, stroke, Type 2 diabetes, and cancer – just to name a few.

Thrills and excitement also release excess dopamine, a chemical inside the brain that causes pleasure and reward, and we want more of it, which makes the game of competition addictive.

Humiliation, worthlessness, and bitterness triggers excess cortisol levels, which increases the risk of high blood pressure, heart attack, stroke, weight gain, depression, Type 2 diabetes, and cancer, etc.

In addition, we think of our competitors as someone against us. In this way, the sword of competition cuts the divine string that connects all human beings, which tarnishes our mental and spiritual health, no matter if we win or lose.

Non-Competitive World

Imagine a world without the sword of competition hanging on everyone's head. The Acquired Self may say, "Oh! How are we going to excel if we don't have competition?"

The fact is that we become far better at our skills when we are free of competitive thoughts. We simply pay full attention to what we do without any emotional thoughts. The best part is that we have no stress and its harmful consequences.

CHAPTER: 18

A GREEDY WORLD

Greed is simply "wanting more." The entire human world is plagued with wanting more money, power, or fame. Often, the three are intertwined.

With few exceptions, everyone wants more. It does not matter which part of the world you live in. Even the spiritual teachers preaching against greed are themselves in the race to get more fame, money and power.

The Root Cause Of Greed

The engine that drives greed is the concept of SUCCESS which gets drilled down into the Acquired Self of almost everyone on the planet. We are programmed from our early childhood to be successful: make a lot of money, be powerful and earn plenty of fame.

It is interesting to note that greed is considered a bad word, while success is a good word. Basically, there is little difference.

Lack Of Contentment

While chasing the phantom of success, we are never satisfied.

Even when we achieve one goal – and experience all the associated thrill and excitement – we are not satisfied. We set up another goal.

What happens if we fail to achieve a goal? We obviously go through the emotional anguish of failure. Often, we don't accept failure and set up another goal. Society admires this type of mindset and calls it a "driven person," which basically is a greedy person.

The natural consequence of greed is lack of contentment. In the grip of greed, we stay dissatisfied, irritated and frustrated, whether we achieve our goal or not.

A greedy person can never be satisfied. No amount of money, power, or fame can ever quench the thirst of greed.

Even a billionaire wants to make more money. Even powerful ones want to grab more power. Most people also want to get more attention, praise, and validation.

Similarly, lack of money, power, and fame also keeps us on the road of greed. In this way, we stay greedy whether we achieve success or fail to achieve success.

In addition, the road of greed is paved with competition, comparison, and ego. Often, there are roadblocks of rules and regulations, which require a lot of physical and mental work. In many situations, bureaucracy, favoritism, corruption, deceptions, and jealousy also get in the cocktail.

Harmful Effects Of Greed On Our Health

Achievements result in thrills and excitement, which give us high adrenaline rush. We also experience a constant state of dissatisfaction, irritation, and frustrations which produce excess amounts of cortisol in addition to adrenaline.

High adrenaline (and noradrenaline) and cortisol levels wreak havoc on our health and puts us at risk of weight gain, Type 2 diabetes, high blood pressure, heart attack, stroke, and cancer – just to name a few.

In addition, competition, comparison, ego, judging, bitterness, frustrations, jealousy, deceptions, and corruption – on the road to success – also cause tremendous harm to our mind and soul.

A World Without Success And Failure

Imagine a world where we work to simply earn our livelihood. Obviously, we are free of the phantom of success and failure and all the associated stress. Then, we are satisfied, content and peaceful.

CHAPTER: 19

A WORLD FULL OF EGO

With rare exceptions, everyone has Ego. What is ego? In its common usage the word ego implies "being special."

Everyone feels special or wants to be special in one way or another. A person is said to have ego if he thinks he is special - better than others.

People usually don't think that they have ego. Instead, they think of themselves as accomplished, successful, gifted, or blessed. These terms are quite *flattering* compared to "ego," which carries a negative connotation.

Basis Of Ego

The Human World downloads ego-making concepts into us as we grow up. These concepts include wealth, success, fame, knowledge, culture, genealogy, heritage, possessions, looks, appearances, religious, political and social affiliations. In the grip of these concepts, we feel special.

EXAMPLES:

- "I" am special because "I" am rich.
- "I" am special because "I" am famous.
- "I" am special because "I" am pretty.
- "I" am special because "I" am a doctor.
- "I" am special because "I" am so cultured.
- "I" am special because "I" am so knowledgeable.

Often people feel special because of their possessions.

EXAMPLES

- "I" feel special because "I" own a special car.
- "I" feel special because "I" own expensive jewelry.
- "I" feel special because "I" own a special pet.
- "I" feel special because "I" own an ancient antique.
- "I" feel special because "I" own designer clothes.

Then there are collective egos. You feel special because you belong to a place, group or community.

EXAMPLES

- "I" am special because "I" live in a certain country, city or neighborhood.
- "I" am special because "I" belong to a certain social, political or religious organization.
- "I" feel special because "My" ancestors were so great.

Ego Of Failure

Ego can take another form that most people are unaware of. Many people get attached to failures, losses, and misery, either due to their own experiences (losses in competition and comparison) or losses of their collective Acquired Self (such as a religious, cultural or political group).

Ego Of Nobility

Sometimes Ego comes from another route. It is the route of nobility. You may decide to become a pious, humble, non-egoic person by reading books of self-improvement or may even go to some retreats which teach you that all evils of the world originate from "power, money, and sex." Then, you develop a negative attachment to "power, money, and sex" and feel you're a better person compared to those who are wealthy, powerful, and sexually desirous.

Harmful Effects Of Ego

All their life, people are either enhancing or defending their ego. In doing so, they create a huge amount of stress for themselves and others. What a waste of life!

Locked in the prison of Ego, people feel quite miserable. On the surface, they are accomplished and successful, but deep inside they feel empty, jealous, and irritated.

You get a momentary thrill and excitement when the Human World makes you feel special by praising your success, special talents, possessions, etc. but soon it fades away… And you want more. You are never satisfied. You can't get enough praise, validation, or recognition. You always want more.

The Human World can't provide you with praise and recognition all the time. Often, it starts criticizing you as well. Then, you feel miserable. You want others, especially your close friends and family members, to like you for your accomplishments and achievements. Instead, they generally may stop liking you because they don't approve of the way you act under the influence of your Ego.

You don't see it that way. You think they're jealous of your success. You often surround yourself with a new set of friends who praise your success. However, inside you keep hurting. Deep down you know that these new friends are fair-weathered friends.

You wish your old friends, and family members would praise you the way your new friends do. Meanwhile, your old friends and family members wish that you'd quit being an egocentric maniac and come back to your senses. The drama goes on and creates a lot of pain and suffering on both sides. Many people resort to vacationing, alcohol, drugs, and many other escapes.

After years of emotional suffering, you decide to "be successful" at relationships, because you hate to be unsuccessful at anything. You may read some books or get advice from professionals. You may even go to a workshop or two and learn a few techniques. However, in the end, nothing seems to work. No one seems to fully understand you or appreciate you for who you are and what you have done for others! People are just so ungrateful and take you for granted, etc.

An egocentric person is in the total grip of their own Acquired Self. They interact with the world from the virtual castle of their own grandiosity. Why and how is this castle of grandiosity built? The Acquired Self builds this virtual castle in the pursuit of emotional security. It wants to suppress the fire of insecurity and worthlessness. It wants to be someone that everyone praises, validates, and acknowledges instead of mocking, humiliating, or criticizing.

For example, as a child or as a teenager you were subjected to comparison or criticism by some authority figure, such as your mother, uncle, or teacher. You felt the pain of humiliation and worthlessness. You also probably felt that you didn't deserve it. They were simply being mean to you. These thoughts of meanness and unfairness provoked intense anger inside you. All these thoughts and emotions get stored in your memory as a constant nagging voice of criticism.

You may not even be aware of these humiliating experiences. Some of these experiences, especially from early childhood, may have been forgotten. However, in your subconscious mind, these experiences are very much alive.

From these humiliating experiences comes another inner thought, "I'll never be humiliated again" or "I'll prove them wrong!" This inner thought becomes your drive to succeed in the world. It makes you work hard. You accomplish a lot, become successful, and earn a lot of money and respect.

You get strongly attached to "success," as it validates you and provide a momentary band-aid on the old, but very much alive, wound of humiliation and anger. Attached to your success, you develop a big ego. On the surface you are accomplished and successful, but inside you still feel worthless, humiliated, angry, and dissatisfied.

You keep working harder, making more money, having more recognition and more power, all of which makes you more egocentric. You expect and hope that now you will never be humiliated again because you are so successful and powerful. However, inside you continue to feel dissatisfied, insecure, worthless, irritated, and angry.

Then, little things bring your inner anger to the surface. You are easily annoyed and have outbursts of anger over things that wouldn't bother other people - things such as someone not agreeing with you or making an innocent, unflattering remark.

Why does this trigger your anger? Because you expect them to acknowledge and validate your success. When they don't, you feel like they are criticizing you and you overreact with all your piled up anger. Unfortunately, this type of behavior causes you to lose some true friends. You want validation from your friends, but your actions push away your true friends. How ironic!

You keep proving to others and yourself how great you are, but it's never enough to heal your inner wound of worthlessness, unfairness, and anger.

In your personal life, any minor disagreement with your spouse or children may send your Acquired Self into a rage. You don't like this hot temper, but you can't help it. You don't even have a clue where it's coming from.

The more successful you become, the bigger your ego becomes and the more easily you get angry over little things.

Some people may not have gone through (or may not remember) humiliating experiences. However, they (their Acquired Self) learn from Society's Collective Acquired Self that success, money, power, or connections with powerful people are very important to live a "successful life" and they start believing in this delusion.

Harmful Effects Of Ego On Health

As pointed out earlier, thrills, excitement, irritations, bitterness, and anger trigger a release of large amounts of adrenaline (and noradrenaline) and cortisol in our body. High adrenaline and cortisol levels put us at risk of high blood pressure, heart attack, stroke, weight gain, Type 2 diabetes, and cancer – just to name a few.

In addition, ego causes tremendous harm to our mind and soul.

Freedom From Ego

Simple realization that it is your Acquired Self, (and not your True Self who creates your ego,) has the power to free you from your ego. *Your Acquired Self is always insecure.* Why? Because it is *virtual, unreal and* really does not exist at all. Hence, it is insecure. So, it seeks virtual security by being *better* than others, by being *special.* The Society Monster provides it with many ideas on how to be *special*. That's how your Acquired Self can thrive inside you.

It is your Acquired Self that generates memories of every event. That's how it keeps them alive and it calls it "My Past." Society's Collective Acquired Self (Society Monster) operates exactly in the same fashion and creates a collective human past in the form of knowledge of history.

By keeping the past alive, the Acquired Self keeps all the pains of humiliation, worthlessness, and unfairness alive and builds a wall of defensive mechanisms around them. These defensive mechanisms, such as competition and comparison, make you respectable, successful, or pious in the eyes of the world.

Your Acquired Self loves these mechanisms because it can get validated through these mechanisms. That's why it never can let go of comparison and competition.

Now what happens if you fully understand all the convoluted working of your Acquired Self? Obviously, you want to *dissociate* yourself from your Acquired Self and with that, your ego automatically vanishes. You realize there is no need to hold on to "your past," because it's not real: it's not happening any longer.

The Past lives only in your head. It does not exist. At the present moment, no one is criticizing or humiliating you through comparison or subjecting you to unfairness. *It happened, but it is not happening at this moment.* No need to build up walls of defensive mechanisms.

You realize that you don't need to feel better than others. In addition, you don't need approval, praise, or validation from others. You realize *life is not a race. Life is to live*!

Everyone is a human being. No one is better than the other and there is no *need* to be better than others. This is the end of the *ego*.

CHAPTER: 20

A WORLD OF LONELINESS

There are a lot of lonely people in the Human World. In general, people can't stand loneliness. They feel bored, worthless, and sad. They may even get depressed.

To run away from loneliness, people find refuge in escapes such as partying, talking on the phone, or staying connected through the internet.

Being lonely implies that you don't have any friends and you're a failure. Many also feel sorry for themselves and get depressed.

Harmful Effects Of Loneliness On Health

Sadness due to loneliness triggers excess cortisol levels, which puts you at high risk of depression, weight gain, type 2 diabetes, high blood pressure, heart attack, stroke, dementia, and cancer, etc.

In addition, loneliness wreaks havoc on your mental health. It can lead to sadness, depression and even suicide.

Loneliness also breaks down the Divine connectivity with everyone else and tarnishes your spiritual health.

The Root Cause of Loneliness

If you want to be free of loneliness, you must take a deeper look at loneliness instead of running away from it.

Psychologically speaking, when you are enslaved by "I, My, Me, Mine," you're separated from every other human being on the planet and of course, you are lonely.

Many people suffer from loneliness, although they may have a large circle of friends. When you're in the grip of "I, My, Me, Mine," you create a psychological wall between yourself and everyone else. Then, you live in a tiny bubble of your own and look through it at everyone else. You obviously feel isolated and lonely but have no clue why you feel this way.

Loss of a loved one is another reason why people sink into the dark hole of loneliness. For example, "I'm lonely because My husband is not with Me." "I'm lonely because My wife passed away."

Escapes From Loneliness

You may hear your inner voice complaining, "no one understands me." Then another voice chimes in. "Loneliness is not a good thing. It's a sign of failure. I must get rid of my loneliness."

Then, you may join a club, party, or organization and become part of their mission which is based on "Us Against Them." In this way, you may become an agitated, competitive, and egocentric person.

Some people may seek the road of partying, alcohol, drugs (legal and illicit), and continue to add stress to their life.

True Freedom from Loneliness

If you want to be free of loneliness, you need to be free of "I, My, Me, Mine." Only then will you start to see things the way they actually are:

- A human being, not My friend or My enemy
- A human being, not My husband or wife.

Then, you realize the next person on the street is another human being, not your friend or your enemy, not a stranger. Automatically, you start talking to people you encounter in grocery stores, restaurants, parking lots, parks, etc. You sense an inner connectedness to every living being on the planet. Loneliness simply evaporates.

CHAPTER: 21

A WORLD OF SELFISHNESS

Almost everyone is selfish in one way or another. Most people work for their own interests. Whenever they deal with other people they ask, “What’s in it for Me?” “Can I make more money?” “Can I have more power, praise and/or sex?” Isn’t that what selfishness is?

A selfish person is always working for their own interests. They may have a long list of things that are important to them. That’s why they have no time for others, including their family and friends.

Selfishness also creates a virtual wall that separates you from the rest of humanity. On the surface, you have plenty of friends, but deep down, you have no friends. You may show superficial signs of friendship, such as sending messages of friendship, meeting for lunch, or joining for some event… But inside, you really don’t care for anyone except for yourself.

When you are selfish, you don’t trust anyone, which is reflected in your relationships. In this way, you have difficulty making sound, healthy relationships. Deep down, you suffer from insecurity, paranoia, and loneliness. You easily get upset when others act in a selfish way. Interesting, isn't it?

Harmful Effects Of Selfishness On Health

Selfishness triggers chronic elevation of cortisol and adrenaline (and noradrenaline), which puts you at high risk of depression, weight gain, type 2 diabetes, high blood pressure, heart attack, stroke, dementia, and cancer, etc.

In addition, selfishness wreaks havoc on your mental and spiritual health.

The Root Cause Of Selfishness

Using logic, let's explore what is at the root of selfishness.

"I, My, Me, Mine Syndrome"

When you're totally in the grip of your Acquired Self, you're operating from its core of "I, My, Me, Mine." Everything revolves around "My interests, My goals, My schedule, My lifestyle, My career, My money, My possessions, etc. It is all about "I, My, Me, Mine" which obviously makes a person selfish.

"We, Us, Our" Syndrome

Often people get attached to a certain social, political, or religious ideology, which then becomes the center of a collective "We, Us, Our" Syndrome. It creates a clannish mentality.

People may work together for their collective interests and may think they are not selfish. However, look deeper and realize that now you're working for the interests of your own "Clan." You are still in the grip of selfishness.

True Freedom From Selfishness

What is this "I, My, Me, Mine?" If you use logic, you realize that it's simply a concept, an idea, an illusion, and nothing more. It's a phantom!

The moment you realize the illusory nature of this "I, My, Me, Mine" you are free from it. Then you see things clearly, as they really are:

EXAMPLES

- A car, not My car
- A house, not My house
- A means to make a living, not My career.
- A human being, not My friend, My enemy, My wife or My husband, My employee or My boss.

- An animal, not My pet.

You get the idea!

With this realization, an incredible freedom from selfishness flows in you. When you're free from "I, Me, My, Mine" you're free from selfishness.

For example, you realize that your wife is a human being, no different from you. She has the same basic needs as you.

You see your employee as human beings just like you. You don't need to keep all the profits for yourself and lie to your employees that your company is losing money.

Once free of a never-ending list of My goals, you have plenty of time for your friends and family members.

Once free from "I, Me, My, Mine" you can truly help someone else, without always thinking "What's in it for Me?" Only then can you be free of your selfish motives. When there is no "I, Me, My, Mine" you don't work for "My interests." This is the end of selfishness!

CHAPTER: 22

A WORLD OF CONDITIONAL LOVE

Love is a word that has several meanings which we learn as we grow up in society. Hence, it is a part of our Acquired Self. This type of love is always *conditional*, based on the concepts in our Acquired Selves, which vary from society to society and from person to person. It can easily change into jealousy, anger, or hate if the *conditions* change.

In contrast, there is love in the domain of the True Self (that we all are born with), which is *unconditional* and *all-encompassing*. It never changes into jealousy, anger, or hate.

Acquired Self Love

The word "love" is something we acquire as we grow up in society. In reality, every word is a sound. It becomes a word when society attaches a concept to the sound. So is the word "love," which has several concepts attached to it.

When I say, "I love you," I am saying that I am deeply attached to you.

When someone says, "I love you," I feel special, appreciated, and validated, which triggers a pleasant emotion.

Strong Positive Attachments

Strong positive attachment to a concept is the basic glue of love. The concept of love comes in many forms, with two broad categories:

- Romantic love
- Non-romantic love

Romantic Love

We are downloaded with the concepts of romance, love, beauty, strength, and desirability, which vary from society to society.

When we reach puberty, our body primes us to engage in sexual acts. However, our society drills down its concept of sexuality: where, when, with whom, and under what conditions is a sexual act permissible.

With the blend of natural sexual desire and societal concepts of romantic love and sexuality, we look for our mate. When we find the right person who fulfills all the conditions, we fall in love. If we're lucky, the other person reciprocates. Now two of us are in love. We feel bonded both in our bedroom and out of the bedroom. We make each other feel special. We care for each other. We get bonded and we feel a warm glow in our hearts.

Non-Romantic Love

There are many other faces of love that make us feel good. Here are a few examples:

- Love of parents and children.
- Love of friendship.
- Love of pets.
- Love of objects such as cars, jewelry, clothes, etc.
- Love of places such as “my home,” “my college,” “my church,” “my country,” etc.
- Love of events such as birthdays, weddings, anniversaries, Christmas, Eid, Diwali, etc.
- Love of money, profession, business, and power.
- Love of appearance.
- Love of sports, music, literature, science, and hobbies, etc.
- Love of TV, newspapers, magazines, computers and internet (such as news, shows, social media, video games, etc.)
- Love of movie stars, musicians, political, and religious leaders, etc.
- Love of an ideology, such as religious, cultural, or political concepts.

The Dark Side Of Love

The love arising out of the Acquired Self is always conditional. Therefore, it readily changes if conditions change. One day you're so close to someone and the next day your relationship falls apart.

For example, the romantic love that compels you to get into a serious relationship (and even marriage) easily changes into anger and hate if you find your partner/spouse has been cheating on you. What happened here? You loved your partner while he/she fulfilled the condition of faithfulness. Once that condition is gone, so is love.

Sometimes, your attachment may be so strong that love changes into possessiveness, which often leads to jealousy, suspicious behavior, and verbal (even physical) violence.

Often the Acquired Self mistakenly starts to believe that a person, object, or place has become part of it. Even the thought of losing that person, object, or place triggers tons of fear. When there is actual loss of the loved one, you get sad and go through a period of grief. The stronger the attachment, the more severe the grief is. Sometimes, it can lead to depression and even suicide.

Sometimes, love is not reciprocated, which leads to a sense of rejection, worthlessness, bitterness, and even revenge.

Strong attachment to career, sports, or a party (political, religious, or cultural) can lead to obsessive compulsive disorder. You also go through emotions of thrills, excitement, bitterness, fear, anger, revenge, and sadness when your beloved sports team or party wins or loses. You experience the same emotional roller coaster with successes, as well as failures, in your career or business that you are so attached to it.

Strong attachment to celebrities creates fans who may become stalkers and cause a lot of stress for the celebrities (and themselves too).

Harmful Effects Of Conditional Love

Conditional love gives you moments of thrills and excitement which triggers large amounts of adrenaline (and noradrenaline) from the adrenal glands.

In addition, emotions arising out of "the dark side of love" such as fear, anger, bitterness, jealousy, worthlessness, and mistrust raise your adrenaline (and noradrenaline) as well as cortisol levels.

High adrenaline (and noradrenaline) and cortisol levels wreak havoc on your health and put you at risk of high blood pressure, heart attack, stroke, weight gain, type 2 diabetes, and cancer – just to name a few.

Sadness from a "broken heart" or grief, primarily raises your cortisol levels, which leads to weight gain, (especially fat storage) and muscle weakness. In addition, sadness decreases serotonin and dopamine levels in the brain, which causes lack of motivation, emotional eating, and profound fatigue. Consequently, you gain more weight, which can make you feel like a failure, which makes you sadder. A vicious cycle sets in which often leads to depression and suicidal ideations.

In addition, emotions arising out of love and "the dark side of love" such as fear, frustrations, anger, bitterness, jealousy, and mistrust cause tremendous harm to our mind and soul.

True Freedom from Conditional Love

Conditional love arises out of your Acquired Self. Therefore, freedom from "conditional" love lies in freedom from the Acquired Self.

Once you are free of "I, Me, My, Mine" you interact with the world in a different way.

You realize you don't own anyone. For example, your spouse is a living person, not your possession. That's the end of expectations, anger jealousy, and mistrust.

Once you are free of the Acquired Self, you are joyful from within. You realize you don't need anyone's love to make you happy. Free of the neediness of love (validation) from others, you become comfortable with your looks, physique, how you talk, walk, dress, etc. That's how insecurity, fear, and associated harmful actions (such as dying your hair to look beautiful for your spouse) comes to an end.

You can never lose anyone (or anything), if you don't own them in the first place. With this simple realization, you are never afraid of losing a spouse, pet, car, house, etc.

If a person dies, you realize that the soul has gone to the other side. If the person was suffering from some chronic illness, (as usually is the case) you realize it must be a great relief for that soul. Instead of being sad at the loss of your loved one, you feel joyfulness of the departing soul.

Once you are free of attachments, life becomes so easy and free of stress. For example, once free of attachment to a sports team, you may enjoy the skills of the players, no matter which side they are on. For you, winning or losing does not matter. That's how you become free of the emotional turmoil of "winning and losing" such as thrills, excitement, disappointments, anger, bitterness, and revenge.

Similarly, if you are not attached to your profession or business, you simply look at it as a way to make a living. Then you are free of greed, fear, and "the emotions of winning and losing."

In short, freedom from the Acquired Self frees you from the trap of conditional love. Then you can be unselfish, emotionally secure, truly joyful. More importantly, you get in touch with True Love that resides inside you.

True Love

True love is not a concept, so you can't grasp it by reading lyrics, poems, or books or watching movies. It does not arise from the "I, Me, My, Mine" of the Acquired Self.

All you have to do is to get out of the grip of your Acquired Self. Then, you will feel it. No words can really describe it.

Love Of Parents And Children

Love between parents and children is a mixture of True love and Conditional Love.

When you lay eyes on your newborn for the first time, you fall in love. This is True Love. You see another human being just like your True Self.

Gradually, your child grows up in society (with your help and guidance) and develops their Acquired Self, which slowly gets in the driver's seat. Then, their Acquired Self interacts with your Acquired Self. Consequently, a layer of Conditional Love develops and covers the layer of True Love, which leads to tons of emotional burden for parents as well as children.

Love Of Friendship

Love of friendship can also be a blend of True Love and Conditional Love.

Generally, we make friends with those who have something in common with our Acquired Self. In this way, it is Conditional Love. It is rooted in mutual respect, caring, expectations, judging, and at times selfishness, jealousy, and control issues. Consequently, most friendships end up creating a lot of emotional stress.

Occasionally, a layer of True Love can surface (as friendship evolves), in the form of deep-seated affection without any selfishness, attachments, expectations, or judging. Then, there is no emotional stress.

Love Of Pets

Love of pets is also a blend of True Love and Conditional Love. Generally, we experience True Love shining through pets and our True Self responds and connects with them.

However, most people get in their Acquired Self and start to train their pets through the tool of reward and punishment. Then, they develop expectations from their pets. They love it when their pet follows their commands and never says "no." In this way, they try to quinch their thirst of *failed* attempts to control the behavior of other human beings. Naturally, their Acquired Self gets a stronger hold over them.

Some dog owners train their dogs well and get into dog shows and competitions." Then, they (and perhaps their dogs as well) go through the emotional roller coaster of "win and lose."

In the grip of their Acquired Self, many pet owners get very attached to their pets. Then, they start to treat them like civilized, conditioned human beings. Pet toilets, birthday parties, fancy clothes and treats are some examples. Some pet-owners allow their pets to sleep with them in their bed at night.

Pets respond to their owners' behavior and get attached to them. Consequently, they suffer from *separation anxiety* if the owner must go on a trip and leave them behind. Similarly, owners suffer tremendously if their pet disappears or dies.

Q: *I want to find love. How can I do it?*

A: Take a closer look at the question. "I" has a desire to find love. Who is this "I?" Of course, it is your Acquired Self who is full of desires. It is always wanting, wishing, desiring. Your Acquired Self wishes to have love, which is a concept, created by Society's Collective Acquired Self. Can you see how the entire question is in the realm of the Acquired Self?

Society's Collective Acquired Self has created all kinds of ways to acquire love. You've probably tried some of those paths but are still looking for love. The whole world is looking for love. This love of the Acquired Self readily changes into hate. This love is not real love, but a phantom, consisting of certain thoughts which trigger certain emotions.

On the other hand, True love is not a concept. It is not some mental destination that you will reach one day by practicing certain techniques.

True love is who you are. It is real. In this way, you are Love. You don't need to search for it. All you need to do is to lift the curtain by freeing yourself from your Acquired Self.

CHAPTER: 23

A WORLD OF HAPPINESS AND SADNESS

The human world is full of happiness and sadness. Sometimes we're happy and at other times, we're sad. We also wish to be happy all the time and never be sad, but happiness is momentary and fleeting. Sooner or later, we fall into the dark hole of sadness, which is also temporary. We continue to ride the rollercoaster of elation and sadness.

The Root Cause of Happiness and Sadness

Let's use logic and look at the cycle of "happiness and sadness" to find real answers.

1.Attachments

When you're happy, who is really happy? It's the "Me" inside you, isn't it? As we observed earlier, "I, My, Me, Mine" creates positive and negative attachments to people, animals, things, concepts, ideologies, etc. Positive attachments give you momentary excitement, which is also called happiness. Loss of positive attachments creates sadness.

For example, you inherit a ring from your beloved grandmother. It's very special to you and has huge sentimental value. Your Acquired Self is positively attached to it. To you, it is not a ring anymore. It is much more than that. It is part of who you are. In fact, it becomes part of your Acquired Self, and you totally identify with your Acquired Self. That's why it makes you happy.

Then one day, you lose your precious ring. You search for it and turn the entire house upside down but can't find it. Your Acquired Self feels utterly sad and unhappy because it has lost a part of itself.

Another example: You love your looks (positive attachment). Your looks become part of "I, My, Me, Mine." "I am beautiful" is what you keep telling yourself. You frequently look at the mirror for verification. Your friends and family also verify that indeed, you are beautiful. Even strangers may validate that you are beautiful. You get recognition, special treatment, and compliments because you are beautiful. All these experiences give you momentary thrills you call happiness.

Then you lose your beautiful looks due to aging or illness. The loss of "My beauty" is a big loss for your Acquired

Self. That obviously creates a huge amount of unhappiness and sadness.

Different people are attached to different things. Most people are attached to money. When you get money, say a bonus at work, a big increase in your stocks, or a jackpot at a casino, you feel thrilled and happy. However, when you lose your job, your stocks go down, or you lose money at a casino, you feel unhappy and sad.

Most people are also attached to their friends and family members. They feel *happy* when they see their favorite family members and close friends and *miss* them when they are not around. They are not ordinary people. They are special because they are a part of "Me." When they die, a part of your Acquired Self dies. A huge loss to your Acquired Self creates unbearable sadness.

Almost everyone is attached to their health. Some are attached to cars, houses, pets, household items, collectible items, clothes, etc. Some are attached to their jobs, achievements, fame, position, etc. Some are attached to ideologies and philosophies.

All these attachments become part of "Me." When you have them, these provide your Acquired Self with moments of happiness. Sooner or later, you lose them and when that happens, your Acquired Self feels bruised because a part of "Me" is not there anymore. That creates a lot of sadness.

2. Competition

Another way to get trapped in the cycle of happiness and sadness is through "competition." In a competition, you may win and that makes you happy or you may lose, and that makes you unhappy.

Competition is one of the basic ingredients of the Human World. Everyone wants to win and be happy, and no one wants to lose and be unhappy.

The software of "win or lose" gets downloaded into your Acquired Self at a very early age with the help of video games, athletic games, board games, spelling bee contests, and beauty competitions, to name just a few.

Each time your Acquired Self, wins, you get happy because your "I" gets validation and praise. Each time it loses, your "I" feel sad.

Harmful Effects Of Happiness And Sadness On Our Health

The thrills and excitement of happiness give us a high adrenaline rush. High adrenaline (and noradrenaline) levels wreak havoc on our physical health and puts us at risk of high blood pressure, heart attack, stroke, diabetes, and cancer – just to name a few.

The thrills and excitement of "Winning" also release excess dopamine, a chemical inside the brain that causes pleasure and reward, and we want more of it, which can make us addicted to sports, video games and gambling.

Humiliation, worthlessness, and sadness triggers excess cortisol levels, which puts us at risk of depression, weight gain, high blood pressure, heart attack, stroke, type 2 diabetes, and cancer, etc.

In addition, attachments and competition seriously tarnish our mental and spiritual health.

True Freedom from the Cycle of Happiness and Sadness

Use logic and you will see that the game of winning and losing is simply a concept, a mental abstraction and is virtual. Unfortunately, you think it's real. That's the illusion. It's only in your head in the form of thoughts, that's all.

Now imagine what happens if a person, whose mind has not been conditioned, watches sports. What he sees is that several people chase and bounce a ball (basketball), carry a ball (rugby), or hit a ball (soccer, baseball, cricket, tennis, golf, ping-pong), etc. He may find it amusing. In the end, he is neither happy nor unhappy, as the concept of victory or defeat doesn't exist in his mind.

Clearly, happiness and sadness are a creation of the conditioned mind, the Acquired Self. Freedom from the Acquired Self automatically frees you from the cycle of happiness and sadness

True Joy

There is a joy that has no opposite. There is always joy, but never any unhappiness or sadness. This true joy does not arise from any attachments or competition. It is not a part of your Acquired Self. In fact, your conditioned mind (your Acquired Self) eclipses this true joy that has resided inside you since your birth. It is part of your True Self.

You see it in newborn babies. It is automatically there once a baby's basic physical needs are met (a full stomach, a clean diaper, and warmth of a blanket or loving arms). It shines through the baby's face. It's there before a baby is attached to anything such as toys or parents. The baby doesn't have to score victories to be happy.

This true joy is still in you. It is not a concept. The conditioned mind can never know it, because it is not a concept. You can feel it once you are free of your conditioned mind, your Acquired Self.

CHAPTER: 24

A WORLD OF DEPRESSION

Depression is a devastating medical condition. You don't feel like doing anything. You simply stay in a sad mood which leads to an overall negative attitude and behavior towards life.

Your negative behavior often cuts you off from those who truly care for you. This makes you more depressed and works as a self-fulfilling prophecy. Sometimes, people become so depressed that they even resort to suicide.

Some so-called spiritual teachers also preach that this world is meant to be full of suffering but after death, the after world will be blissful. This kind of thinking may appeal to a depressed person who may end up committing suicide.

Bipolar Affective Disorder

Some people go through periods of low energy as a part of depression, followed by periods of high nervous energy due to underlying anxiety disorder. This is called Bipolar Affective Disorder.

Drug Treatment Of Depression

Most people take medications to treat symptoms of depression. Often, they stay on these drugs forever or their symptoms relapse.

Drugs are a superficial approach to treat depression. With the passage of time, patients usually need to change their drug or add more drugs to manage their depressive symptoms.

Anti-depression drugs also have serious side-effects. To deal with these side-effects, you end up on more drugs. Before you know it, you are on a long list of medicines, dealing with their side effects.

Harmful Effects Of Depression

In addition to what is already discussed, depression also increases levels of cortisol, which often leads to excessive weight gain, muscle weakness, weak bones, heart attack, high blood pressure, type 2 diabetes, stroke, dementia, and cancer.

What Is The Root Cause Of Depression?

Society tells you that depression is due to a chemical imbalance (such as low levels of serotonin) in your brain. Therefore, you will have to take anti-depression drugs to control your depression for the rest of your life.

The fact is that the chemical imbalance in the brain is simply the *mechanism* and *not* the root cause of depression. One must think, what caused the chemical imbalance? The root cause of chemical imbalance is your own *negative* thinking.

Why does a person feel depressed? Sometimes, it is due to an incident, event, or situation, such as loss of a loved one. Sometimes, you get a chronic illness, or you're in a bad situation at work or at home and there is no way out. Often, you don't even know why you are depressed.

When you say, "I am depressed," who is this "I" who is depressed? This "I" is your Acquired Self, isn't it? While you completely identify with your Acquired Self, you will continue to be depressed.

Another reason for depression is your memories. Your Acquired Self contains piles and piles of memories, bad as well as sweet, both of which can be at the root of your depression. Bad memories obviously create a lot of psychological pain for you. How about sweet memories? Well, sweet memories are the basis of "missing." For example, you love your daughter and have a lot of fond memories. Now she has grown up and moved away. Stuck in those sweet memories, you start to miss her. Sometimes "missing" can lead to depression.

Memories are the root cause of depression. Therefore, let's examine what a memory really is. A memory is a snapshot of an event, with a story attached, an interpretation/judgment and a corresponding emotion. In this way, memories are created by your own Acquired Self and therefore, it holds on to them as "My" memories and keeps them alive.

For example, you were humiliated in front of your class by your 2nd grade teacher. The event is long gone, but you still have a vivid picture of the entire event and can still feel the pain of humiliation. The event has died, but it is very much alive in your head with all of its fire of psychological pain.

Now consider this. Events are happening all the time. Your Acquired Self keeps making memories out of these events. Imagine the heavy burden of memories your Acquired Self has graciously generated for you. Within these memories lie your emotions of worthlessness, sadness, loneliness, embarrassment, and abandonment.

A bubbling volcano of these emotions creates chemical changes in your brain. Then, the altered chemical environment is conducive to more negative thoughts. These negative thoughts then trigger more negative emotions and consequently, more negative thoughts, which results in a vicious cycle of negative thoughts, negative emotions and associated chemical changes in the brain. This is what causes depression. It all starts with negative thoughts, which then lead to negative emotions and subsequent chemical changes in the brain.

Anti-depression drugs work by counteracting the chemical changes in your brain, but do *not* take care of the root cause: the thoughts which are kept alive as memories by your Acquired Self. ***An analogy is swatting mosquitoes while the pond continues to widen.*** That's why you end up adding more drugs as time goes by, to control your symptoms of depression.

It is worth noting that some painful events from your early childhood get so deep into your Acquired Self that you may not even recollect them, but they stay alive in your unconscious mind, a part of your Acquired Self. On the other hand, you can easily recollect many events.

Your subconscious mind – is another part of your Acquired Self.

Hope As An Escape Mechanism

To escape from the relentless agony of memories, your mind can generate some positive thoughts, it calls hope. In this way, it can temporarily stop the vicious cycle of negative thoughts, and negative emotions. However, hope creates the so-called future and is often a temporary remedy. Sooner or later, your memories take over and you become depressed again. Many people go through swings of hopefulness and hopelessness.

"Stay Busy" As An Escape Mechanism

You may be advised to stay busy to ward off depression. Society has created proverbs such as "an empty mind is the devil's workshop." By staying busy, you may be trying to run away from your memories. However, this escape mechanism also does not work for long. Sooner or later, you get stuck in your memories and become depressed again.

Other Escape Mechanisms

To find some relief from the agony of memories, your Acquired Self can run to some other "escapes" as well. These escapes can take the form of excessive eating, excessive work, excessive partying, excessive alcohol, excessive sex, illegal drugs, smoking, pornography, gambling, etc. Each escape has its own negative consequences. Obviously, these escapes do not free you from your painful memories.

True Freedom From Depression

Once you fully understand that the root cause of your depression is your own Acquired Self, you stop running for "escapes." Instead, you feel empowered that the solution lies inside you. All you have to do is to be free of your Acquired Self.

Clearly see the virtual nature of your memories. Yes, events happened, but those events are not happening any more except in your head. New events happen all around you all the time, but you remain so trapped in your memories that you miss out on most events in the Now such as the gentle breeze, the chirping birds, and the twinkling stars.

Live in the Now and pay attention to the real events happening around you in your field of awareness which is: what you see, hear, smell, taste and touch. ***The moment your memories don't have your attention, they cease to exist in that moment.*** That's how you get freedom from your memories. The more you stay in the Now, the more you will stay away from your memories.

Every now and then you may find yourself in the grip of your memories. However, then you will see the true nature of these memories: They are virtual, illusory, unreal. No more than bundles of thoughts and emotions. You will not believe in anything these memories imply. Why? Because none of those events are happening right now. Hence, there is no need to run away, or change or make sense out of those events from the so called "past." Just see them for what they are: ghosts swirling in your head. That's all!

Once you stop the stream of negative thoughts, your brain starts to heal and the chemical changes in the brain (neurotransmitters such as low serotonin) reverse themselves. In addition, you can accelerate this process of healing by full intention that you (as a part of the Divine) have the ultimate healing power to heal anything including depression. That's how your depression automatically ends.

Caution: Please do not stop any medicine without consulting your doctor.

CHAPTER: 25

A WORLD OF EMBARRASSMENT AND SHAME

Many people suffer from embarrassment and shame. Consequently, they feel bad inside. Often, there is an underlying sense of failure, guilt, humiliation, and worthlessness.

What Is The Basis Of Embarrassment And Shame?

As you grow up, you pick up a lot of ideas along the way including what's right and what's wrong; what's desirable and what's not; what's acceptable and what's not. You also learn a lot of *manners* to observe when interacting in society. That's how you acquire your Acquired Self.

Equipped with this information, your "Acquired Self" judges others. It also knows that others are judging it as well. If you or someone close to you, (say your child), falls below the standards set by society, your Acquired Self feels embarrassed and ashamed.

Examples:

- Your ten-year-old daughter doesn't listen to you in front of your friends. You feel ashamed, because you *failed* to teach her the manners of "respecting your elders."
- When your husband starts talking loud after a couple of drinks, you feel embarrassed and ashamed because you feel as if you married a *loser*.
- You go to a party without having proper attire. You feel embarrassed, because deep down, you feel *ignorant* or *poor*.
- You go to a restaurant or a club by yourself and feel uneasy, thinking others may judge you to be a *loser* who has no friends.
- You arrive late to a party because traffic was horrible. You feel embarrassed and apologetic because you think others might judge you to be a *rude* person.
- While having a dinner conversation, you didn't know some historic facts (or some other knowledge), which made you feel embarrassed, knowing that others may think you are an *ignorant* person.

Your Acquired Self wants to be *accepted* by other members of society. An intense desire to be part of society is to cover up your deep-rooted insecurity. The larger the insecurity, the more you cling to manners and standards of society. You see this behavior – in its extreme form – at "high society" country clubs, where you're judged by if you wore the proper tie and shoes with your suit or if you used the right utensils during dinner.

Deeply caught up in your Acquired Self, you feel extremely sensitive to anything less than perfect (according to the club rules) and you get easily embarrassed.

Moments of embarrassment and humiliation get stored in your memory box and create a huge amount of shame and unworthiness. These memories then generate further thoughts that this embarrassment should not happen in the future. That's why you develop a *fear* of embarrassment as well.

Harmful Effects Of Embarrassment And Shame

Embarrassment and shame triggers excess release of cortisol and adrenaline (and noradrenaline), which puts you at high risk of weight gain, Type 2 diabetes, infections, cancer, heart attack, high blood pressure, stroke, and dementia.

In addition, embarrassment and shame harm your mental and spiritual health.

True Freedom From Embarrassment And Shame

If only people knew the root cause of embarrassment and shame, they could be free of it in a moment. The simple realization that embarrassment and shame is not part of your True Self, but part of your Acquired Self, is very liberating. Then, you can truly let go of it. Just imagine the relief you get just knowing all the embarrassment and shame you harbor is not the true you, but all of it was shoved down your throat in the name of *manners* and *culture*.

Freedom from the tight grip of the Acquired Self liberates you from the cage of embarrassment and shame.

CHAPTER: 26

A WORLD OF COMPLAINERS

Have you observed how people complain all the time? Complaining is so prevalent that most people aren't even aware they're complaining. It seems like a normal way of thinking.

EXAMPLES:

- I don't like this weather.
- I don't like my job.
- I don't like living in this area.
- I don't like this culture.
- I don't like mathematics.
- I don't like greedy people.
- I don't like this music.
- I don't like my looks.
- I don't like my husband.
- I don't like what's happening in the world.
- I don't like Muslims, Christians, Hindus, etc.
- I don't like Latinos, Asians, whites, blacks, etc.

- I don't like Russians, Canadians, Germans, Irish, French, etc.
- I don't like deserts, forests, or snow, etc.
- I didn't like the service I got.
- I didn't like my history teacher.
- I didn't like the food that was served.

Various Forms Of Complaining

Complaining is basically an expression of non-acceptance. Different people express it differently. Some people use strong negative words in a loud voice, while others may put a sarcastic tone to it. Some people express it politely, chit-chatting with their friends. Some may not express it out loud but keep talking about it in their head. Many people express it through their gestures, writings, and actions.

Harmful Effects Of Complaining

Complaining triggers high adrenaline (and noradrenaline) and cortisol levels, which wreaks havoc on our physical health and puts us at risk of high blood pressure, heart attack, stroke, dementia, Type 2 diabetes, and cancer – just to name a few.

In addition, complaining affects our emotional health and tarnishes our spiritual wellbeing.

Root Cause of Complaining

When someone complains, who is actually complaining? If you pay attention, you will realize it is always "I" who complains. Who is this "I?" Isn't it your Acquired Self? It does *not like* what is happening or what has already happened. Often it does not like certain people, events, concepts, objects, or even nature such as the weather.

When the Acquired Self says, "I don't like," it is judging, isn't it? From early childhood, your Acquired Self learns to *judge* every person, object, situation, event, philosophies, etc., based on information and concepts that are stored in it. Examples include how someone should and shouldn't behave or how things should or shouldn't be or who is a good person, who is a bad person, good weather, bad weather, etc.

A Cloud Of Negativity

Each time you complain, verbally or mentally in your head, your Acquired Self triggers negative emotions with serious consequences for your body. By complaining, your Acquired Self is trying to assert itself as being right (and someone else as wrong).

For example, you tell your story to your friends, trying to get sympathy from their Acquired Selves which they gladly provide. In addition, they reinforce your complaint with their own stories. Soon you have several stories centered on how someone (or a group of people), or someplace or something is wrong. In this way, these Acquired Selves find something in common and feel bonded. In fact, all of you have produced negativity not only for yourself, but also for everyone around you, a cloud of negativity. This is how victim mentality is produced.

Sometimes, it may not be your own experience, but the experience of someone you have never met. Next time, in a social situation, just examine how one person starts complaining in a polite way. For example, someone shares news read in the newspaper or heard on TV centered around someone's complaint. Soon, several Acquired Selves tell their own stories (or stories they read or watched on the news.) If you pay attention, you can feel the heaviness of the field of negativity.

Freedom From Complaining

Use logic and you can clearly see that complaining is a common pastime of your Acquired Self. Once you are free of the Acquired Self, you automatically stop judging. Then, you are free from the useless, toxic, energy-draining habit of complaining.

In a social setting, when people start to create a cloud of negativity, gently switch the topic to something pleasant, instead of falling into the rabbit hole of complaining.

Sensible Actions

It doesn't mean you can't point out if something is wrong or someone did something wrong to you. Once you are free of your habit of complaining, you can clearly mention your point of view as a "matter of fact." This type of action does not arise out of negativity and does not have a fighting tone to it. You may be surprised to see that this non-emotional tone is much more effective than the negative tone.

Furthermore, if some situation is *physically* unpleasant such as hot weather, take some sensible action instead of just complaining about it. Many people just keep complaining without taking any action, which of course continues to perpetuate their negative attitude.

Some situations may not allow you to take any action for the time being. Accept things as they are until you can act. For example, I know several people who frequently complain about harsh winters in Canada, but don't take any action to relocate from Canada to some warmer place. They give plenty of reasons why they cannot relocate. I advise them to simply accept cold winters and stop complaining about them.

CHAPTER: 27

A WORLD OF LIARS

The Human World is full of liars. Often people come up with more lies to cover up their previous lies. In this way, they dig themselves into a deep hole of lies.

People lie for a variety of reasons. Some lie to deceive and manipulate - others for their own selfish motives. Some lie to cover up "wrongdoing," and are afraid of being caught. Some lie to boost their ego. They may exaggerate simple facts to impress other people. Then, there are trivial, harmless lies.

Some liars become defensive and vindictive and try to fight back at the person who caught their lie.

Harmful Effects Of Lying

Liars may suffer from fear and anxiety of being caught. Many liars suffer from selfishness, greed, and ego-enhancement.

People who are lied to suffer a lot. They become disenchanted, disappointed, and deeply hurt. They may even get angry. In this way, lying erodes trust forever.

All these emotions (fear, selfishness, greed, ego-enhancement, disappointment, and anger) adversely affect our physical, mental, and spiritual health, as we observed earlier.

The Root Cause Of Lying

Why do people lie? Mostly because they have done something "bad" and are afraid of being caught. Why are they afraid of being caught? Because they will be punished if they get caught. Obviously, they don't want to be punished, therefore they lie.

Who is it in you that lies? It's your Acquired Self, isn't it? You are not born with it. You acquire the concepts of "bad behavior, punishment, and avoiding pain" as you grow up in society. As a result of these concepts, you start lying.

For example, as a child you did something that your parents' thought was wrong. Let's say you hid your brother's shoes just for fun. They asked if you did it and you said, "yes." Then, you got punished for it. Your memory stored the entire event as pain arising out of admission of wrongdoing.

Your Acquired Self learns from its mistake and generates another thought in your subconscious: I will avoid pain by never admitting any wrongdoing. In school, you do wrong things but never admit it. You not only get away with pranks, but maybe the other kids start to think of you as a sneaky genius. You may become a habitual liar.

Society further enhances lying habits by rewarding some liars. For example, lawyers lie all the time and get paid well for their brilliant work. They also strongly advise you to never admit any wrongdoing. Similarly, politicians lie all the time and enhance their political career in this way.

When you get caught lying, you feel embarrassed, ashamed, and guilty. Obviously, it causes a lot of emotional pain for you. Therefore, you might try to seek some help, usually in the form of counseling from a friend, a professional or a book. It may work for a while, but before you know it, you're repeating the whole cycle all over again.

True Freedom From Lying

Can there be true freedom from lying? You need to ask this question yourself. My answer is Yes.

Fear, selfishness, greed, and ego are the root causes of lying behavior. As noted earlier, these are various components of the Acquired Self. A person lies if they are totally in the grip of their Acquired Self.

Once you are free of your Acquired Self, you are free of fear, ego, selfishness, and greed. Only then, your actions that arise are not bad at all. Then, there is no fear of being caught and obviously, there is no need to lie. Also, the need to boost ego vanishes. Similarly, freedom from greed liberates you from manipulating people for selfish gains of money and power.

Freedom from the Acquired Self truly liberates you from the need to lie.

Harmless Lies

Sometimes, you may lie to protect yourself. For example, you may decide *not* to give out accurate personal information if it is not necessary, such as filling out some online form or signing an attendance sheet at a conference, etc. Often, personal information is sold for profit. Even worse, fraudulent people try to steal your identity, which is quite common these days.

Therefore, always use common sense and be practical.

CHAPTER: 28

A WORLD OF PREJUDICES

What is prejudice? In simple terms, we are prejudiced when we judge people negatively with our preconceived notions.

What Is The Root Cause Of Prejudice?

Why are we prejudiced? Because we want to subdue (in a civilized way), those who are not like us. It arises from the concept of "Us Against Them." Deep down, we are afraid of them, based on historical information downloaded in our Acquired Self.

What is history? It is simply opinions of historians with their own prejudice, isn't it? Instead of looking at the root cause, historians get consumed by details and (superficial) reasons for conflicts and wars.

The Collective Human Past is littered with cruelties humans have inflicted on each other in the name of religion, nationalism, and race, to name a few.

Why did these cruelties happen? These cruelties occurred because humans are divided along lines of concepts such as religion, race, and nationalism. If we truly want to end these cruelties, shouldn't we rise above these emotional divisions?

In the grip of the Acquired Self, we are afraid "what if" history repeats itself. Out of this fear, we get alarmed about the potential rise of our old enemies who are now living among us, as we are now a civilized world. Instead of openly waging wars, we want to subdue them with our prejudice.

Harmful Effects Of Prejudices

People who hold prejudices often experience stress in the form of fear. In addition, victims of prejudice go through anger, resentment, and hate.

As we observed earlier, these emotions adversely affect our physical, emotional, and spiritual health.

True Freedom From Prejudices

We can experience people as they really are, only if we are free of the preconceived ideas stored up in our Acquired Self. Then, we see a person as a human being, not as Caucasian, African American, Asian, Christian, Muslim, Hindu, Jewish, English, Hispanic, American, French or Chinese. Prejudices automatically die out.

CHAPTER: 29

A WORLD OF JEALOUSY

Jealousy is a gnawing emotion. It kills any peace of mind you have. A jealous person is in constant psychological pain. It's a sign of failure and bad character to be jealous, isn't it?

The Root Cause Of Jealousy

If you pay attention, you realize jealousy arises out of your own inner voice:

- "I deserve what she has."
- "Why him and not me?"
- "Why does he have everything and not Me? I'm the one who really deserves to have a loving spouse, mansion, fame, praise, validation, and recognition."

There is a deep-seated sense of lack of praise, recognition, and validation. Also, there are underlying emotions of disappointment and unfairness.

It's all about "I, My, Me, Mine," isn't it? It's your Acquired Self who is jealous. The Acquired Self is conditioned to be competitive. It wants to win and never lose. It wants to be praised, validated, and acknowledged by others. Therefore, it works hard to win, to be better than others, and expects validation. However, when it doesn't get what it expects, it gets deeply hurt. Instead, someone else gets success, recognition, and validation. "How unfair" says your Acquired Self.

Harmful Effects Of Jealousy

Jealousy triggers high levels of adrenaline (and noradrenaline) and cortisol, which adversely affects our physical, emotional, and spiritual well-being, as observed earlier.

True Freedom From Jealousy

The moment you realize that you are not your Acquired Self, you become free of the neediness to be praised and acknowledged. You realize that your True Self existed before you were lured into the game of competition and comparison. You realize the conceptual nature of "win and lose, praise and reward." That's how jealousy simply ends.

CHAPTER: 30

A WORLD OF HYPOCRISY

We call someone a hypocrite if they pretend to be nice, moral, and virtuous, but in fact, they are *not*. A person deceives when they are being hypocritical.

It is interesting to note that a hypocritical person does not see themself as a hypocrite, although others may clearly see it. Why? Because the word hypocrite carries a negative connotation. These people consider themselves to be polite, nice, and diplomatic - much better words than hypocritical.

What Is The Root Cause Of Hypocrisy?

To be free of hypocrisy, we need to look deeper at it instead of running away from it. First, we need to admit that we are hypocritical. Only then can we go deeper.

Who is it inside you who *pretends* to be nice, polite, and moral? It's your Acquired Self, isn't it? What is nice, polite, and moral? Concepts, right? Do newborn babies pretend to be polite, nice, and moral? Obviously *not*.

The concepts of nice, polite, and morales get downloaded into your Acquired Self, along with many other concepts as you grow up in society. Greed, selfishness, anger, hate, bitterness, revenge, bias, prejudice, violence, addiction, self-righteousness, fear, and jealousy are some of the products of these concepts.

In other words, society trains your Acquired Self to be greedy, selfish, hateful, revengeful, and prejudiced. At the same time, it teaches your Acquired Self to *be* polite, nice, and moral. Obviously, these are conflicting concepts. Therefore, you pretend to be nice, polite, and moral while your actions speak the other way, filled with greed, selfishness, and prejudices.

True Freedom From Hypocrisy

Once you fully understand the root cause of hypocrisy, will you still be hypocritical? Obviously *not*. Once you realize you are not your Acquired Self, you are free of the concept of "nice, polite and moral." At the same time, you also get freedom from greed, selfishness, anger, hate, revenge, jealousy, fear, bias, and prejudice. Then, you become a truly nice, kind, and virtuous person *without trying* to be one. This is how hypocrisy automatically ends.

CHAPTER: 31

A WORLD OF GRIEF

Grief is a deep sense of loss, usually loss of someone or something very *close* to you. It could be the death of a loved one. It could be the loss of a possession such as your precious jewelry, car, or house. It could be loss of your job, savings, or pension plan. It could be the loss of your friendship, marriage, or your political or religious philosophy.

Grief is quite painful. It can take various forms such as utter shock, anger, profound sadness, and guilt. Many people can't stand it and end up getting depressed. Some may try to suppress these emotions through denial and eventually end up with *emptiness, restlessness,* and *anxiety*. Some try various escape mechanisms, which are only temporary fixes and often cause more trouble.

Harmful Effects Of Grief

Grief triggers high levels of cortisol which adversely affects our physical, emotional, and spiritual well-being, as discussed earlier.

True Freedom From Grief

Use logic and you realize that grief comes from the loss of someone or something that you were very attached to and had become an integral part of "you." In fact, what you think is "you," is not the real you, but is actually your Acquired Self. Therefore, it is your Acquired Self that is *bruised,* because part of it is gone or taken away.

The moment you disassociate yourself from your Acquired Self, you will feel relief from grief.

Pay attention to the *Now*, your field of awareness. Experience life inside you and around you that is filled with joy. Then, you realize you are part of the *Now.* You feel an amazing inner peace and joy. This is your True Self!

When you are in the light of your True Self, emotions of grief simply dissipate. You realize you don't own anyone or anything. Obviously, you don't lose your loved one, because you didn't own them in the first place. You also realize your loved one did not just come to a dead end but passed on to the other side.

CHAPTER: 32

A WORLD OF MISTRUST, PARANOIA, PSYCHOSIS

What is trust? What do you really mean when you say, "I trust you?" Don't you imply that I expect you to behave in certain ways and *not* to behave in certain other ways? In this way, trust implies expectations at a deep level. For example, if I tell my child, "I trust you to finish your homework," what I really mean is that I expect her to finish her homework or I will be seriously disappointed. When you trust someone, you basically expect a certain kind of behavior from them.

Your expectations are very *deep* when you trust someone, and therefore, if your expectations are not met, you get hurt *deeply*. For example, if your trusted friend betrays you, it is more hurtful than if some colleague doesn't live up to your expectations.

Trust is one of the foundations of marriage. You expect your spouse to be faithful. However, if your spouse cheats on you, you are badly hurt.

What Is The Root Cause Of Lack Of Trust

Let's take a close look at the origin of deep expectations and trust. These deep expectations start in our early childhood.

Babies start to trust their parents, because they are always there to fulfill their needs, physical as well as psychological. Now, what happens if one day you decide to leave your little one in the care of a babysitter? Your baby cries and cries. What happens? Trust is *broken,* as your baby feels *abandoned*. Therefore, she cries and cries. After a few hours, you are back.

Now you are again there to fulfill all her physical as well as psychological needs, until the next episode of "babysitting." Your baby's trust (in you) gets restored, although not completely, because the previous traumatic experience of *abandonment* is simply pushed down into the unconscious.

You may also have to go out of town as a part of your job. Some parents must leave their children for days, months or even years, to earn a living for the family.

Parents think they are making a sacrifice for the family, but their children do not understand this sacrifice. All they know is that their loving dad (or mom) is not around to spend time with them. They trusted you to be there, but you broke their trust.

As your child grows up, sooner or later you want to discipline your child for bad behavior. You may use harsh words. Your child's Acquired Self is deeply hurt, because they trusted you to be a *loving* person. "How could you hurt me while I trusted you to love me?" an inner voice silently questions.

The more your child is attached to you, the more they are going to get hurt each time you break their trust by abandoning or punishing them, which often leads to piles of resentment, anger, and revenge.

The repeated episodes of *trust shattering experiences* continue to pile up into the Acquired Self at the unconscious and subconscious level and remain very much *alive* there, although a person may or may not remember them.

Consequently, a person with a heavy load of this kind of emotional experience may never be able to engage in a truly trusting relationship with a spouse, child, neighbor, coworker, or community.

Paranoia

Lack of trust can take a more severe form to the point that a person not only mistrusts someone but also becomes suspicious of them. This we call *paranoia.*

Overly protective parents – in the grip of their own Acquired Selves – download *suspicion* into the growing Acquired Self of their children. Phrases such as "Never trust any stranger. They may harm you," are commonly used by parents who themselves suffer from paranoia. In this way, paranoia (and psychosis) may sound genetically transmitted, but it is mostly the result of upbringing.

Psychosis

In the grip of the Acquired Self, such a person looks at others with suspicion and may even start to *believe* that others are, in fact, out there to harm them. This leads to *delusional thinking,* which may then affect the behavior of these individuals.

These people start to protect themselves from their own mind-made dangers and threats.

Often such a person avoids social interactions, as the mind is overwhelmed with suspicious thoughts. From these thoughts, more convoluted and delusional thoughts arise, based upon what else lies in the contents of the Acquired Self. For example, a person may declare they are *talking to God* or acting under the *directions of God*. Sometimes, the thoughts can be so overwhelming that a person may start seeing or hearing imaginary things or events. This we label as *"hallucinations*." Actions arising out of delusions and hallucinations can harm oneself or others.

This kind of severely abnormal, delusional thinking, and totally irrational behavior is what we label as "Psychosis."

Delusions and hallucinations are created by the Acquired Self, and such a person completely identifies with their Acquired Self. Therefore, to that person, these delusions and hallucinations are real, although everyone else can see they are unreal and imaginary.

True Freedom From Mistrust And Paranoia

If you seriously want to be rid of mistrust and paranoia, you must look deeply. What is at the root of these psychological disorders? If you dig deeply, you will find that the culprit is the Acquired Self: the conditioned mind, emotional experiences and thoughts swirling in the head.

To be free of mistrust and paranoia, you must be free of your Acquired Self. Only then will you realize that all the mistrust, anger, and suspicion is only in your conditioned mind, keeping you away from reality. Simply use logic and you can be free of your Acquired Self. Then, there are no expectations, no trust or mistrust, no suspicion, no enemies, no one to be afraid of. In this way, you can be free of mistrust and paranoia.

True Freedom From Psychosis

When a person is in the tight grip of their Acquired Self and completely identifies with it, they get totally lost in their thoughts and emotions. They lose touch with reality and live in a *virtual world* of their own. This is the basis of psychosis.

Is it possible to be free of psychosis? In my opinion, it is possible but extremely difficult. In most cases, it can only be managed with medications, which help them be able to function (to a degree) in society. More importantly, medical treatment prevents them from hurting themselves or others.

Note: Please do not stop taking your medications without the advice of your doctor.

CHAPTER: 33

A WORLD OF RELIGIONS

Like other concepts, the human mind has also created various concepts about the Divine. Hence, there are various religions, each claiming to be the right path to the Divine.

Impact Of Religions

Religions are a strong force that shape the Human World, with all their good and bad influences. For example, religious centers are a place for socialization. In addition, religions typically help those who are less fortunate, powerless, and struggling with emotional health.

On the other hand, religions are divisive and create "Us Against Them," which is the basis of most human conflicts.

Religions are also in a race of power and money.

While many people have positive attachment to religious spirituality, some have negative attachment to this concept. They call themselves atheists.

Harmful Effects Of Strong Attachment To Religions on Health

As we observed earlier in the book, the concept of "Us Against Them," and the race for power and money, triggers an excessive release of adrenaline (and noradrenaline) and cortisol, which puts you at a high risk of weight gain, Type 2 diabetes, infections, cancer, heart attack, high blood pressure, stroke, and dementia, to name a few.

Freedom From Religions

Use common sense - our innate intelligence - to see clearly. To see the mind of the Creator, see its creation: the newborn baby. No baby comes into this world and declares that they are Christian, Muslim, Hindu, Jewish, etc.

Once free of the conceptual world – The Acquired Self – we get in touch with our True Self, the self that reflects True Divine: love, peace, and joy for all, free of any conditions and divisions.

CHAPTER: 34

A WORLD OF MORALITY AND IMMORALITY

The Human Conceptual World was created by Society's Collective Acquired Self. It wants to control everyone's behavior, which is the foundation for the concept of morality. The basic intention is to keep society running orderly. However, often it does not work out that way. In fact, it also creates many social as well as emotional issues.

Book Of Morality

Various parts of the Human World have created their own "book of morality." It describes how everyone in that society should and should *not* behave. Often, these concepts are borrowed from the prevalent religion in that society.

All these concepts get downloaded into the Individual Acquired Self as we grow up in society.

Consequences Of The Book Of Morality

As a result of the concepts of morality, most people create tons of emotional stress for themselves and others.

Judging

The concept of morality is the basis of constant judging we all do. Few examples: A bad person, a good fellow, a good husband, a bad husband, a good wife, a bad wife, a good friend, a bad friend, etc. Judging someone good or bad triggers a corresponding *good or bad* emotion.

Self-criticism

The concept of morality is also the basis of self-criticism which can trigger the gnawing emotion of guilt.

Expectations

The concept of morality creates expectations, which can give rise to disappointments, sadness, annoyances, jealousy, anger, and hate.

Rules, Regulations and Laws

Society also creates rules, regulations, and laws from its concept of morality. Then, it enforces these concepts through the power of "reward and punishment." We get *rewarded* if we ***do** what society wants*. We get *punished* if we ***do not do** what* *society wants*. We can also get *punished* if we *do what society does **not want*** **us to do**.

However, the system of reward and punishment is not black and white. It is often corrupted by favoritism, power, and money.

In short, "morality, rules, regulations, and laws" are important tools that are meant for society to function in an orderly manner, although they often fail to do so. They also end up creating immense emotional stress for everyone.

Harmful Effects Of Morality On Health

A strong attachment to morality wreaks havoc on your physical, emotional, and spiritual health.

As we observed earlier in the book, expectations, judging and self-criticism trigger excessive release of adrenaline (and noradrenaline) and cortisol, which puts you at high risk of weight gain, Type 2 diabetes, infections, cancer, heart attack, high blood pressure, stroke, and dementia, to name a few.

Freedom From Morality

Once we clearly see "morality, rules, regulations, and laws" as a concept, we feel so liberated. We stop judging others or ourselves. We try to do the right thing, but we have no expectations from others. Hence, no disappointments, sadness, annoyances, jealousy, anger, or hate. We are also not afraid anymore.

Note:

We must recognize "morality, rules, regulations, and laws" as important tools for us to function in society. We must follow them but not be in the grip of them.

CHAPTER: 35

A WORLD OF ADDICTIONS

Addiction affects most of us to a degree. It is only when it becomes excessive and undesirable that we, as a society, call it addiction.

Addictions can take various forms such as compulsive eating, excessive smart phone/computer use, smoking, excessive work, excessive TV watching, excessive video games, excessive golfing, excessive alcohol, excessive gambling, excessive illegal drugs.

It's interesting to note that Society's Collective Acquired Self has singled out certain excessive behaviors as *addictions* and others as *accomplishments*. For example, a businessman seeking excessive excitement by making more money and not spending time with his wife and children is called an accomplished, honorable person. On the other hand, a person seeking excessive excitement by using recreational drugs is considered a bad person and a failure. If you think logically, they are both addicted, one to money and the other to recreational drugs.

The Root Cause Of Addiction

In most cases, *competition, comparison, judging, and guilt* are at the root of addictions.

In the game of *competition*, you either win or lose. If you win, you get "*thrill and excitement,*" but it is short-lived and you want more of it.

What happens if you lose in a competition? It leads to emotions of unworthiness and sadness. At times, it also causes a sense of *unfairness, self-pity, bitterness, anger and jealousy.*

Comparison makes "someone better than others" or "someone worse than others."

Judging is based on the concepts downloaded into our Acquired Self, such as concepts of beauty and ugliness, intelligence and stupidity, good and bad, wealth and poverty, etc.

Now what happens when you are told that you are "better than" or you are "the best" or "the most beautiful?" Obviously, you feel praised, validated, and special. They boost your ego and you want more of these compliments.

What happens when you are told that you are "worse than" or "the worst" or even "dumb and stupid?" Obviously, you feel worthless, humiliated, and sad. You do not want to hear those kinds of comments!

Judging also gives rise to *"guilt."* As we observed earlier in the book, the root cause for guilt is self-criticism, which is the result of the "book" of values, traditions, morality, and ethics downloaded into your Acquired Self. You judge yourself (and everyone else) through the filters of these concepts. What happens if on some occasion, or in a certain situation, you can't live up to these concepts? Obviously, you feel guilty for the rest of your life.

Victories, praises, and validations bring momentary "thrill and excitement" to your Acquired Self - *but it wants more of it*. It becomes *addicted* to the moments of thrill and excitement. The pursuit of *more* makes you greedy and you are never satisfied.

Therefore, you live in a psychological state of dissatisfaction, agitation, and nervousness even when you are winning. Consequently, you may seek out more momentary thrills and excitement through recreational drugs, alcohol, gambling, etc.

On the other hand, your Acquired Self also holds on to the psychological pain of humiliation, worthlessness, unfairness, anger, revenge, and guilt. As this pain becomes intolerable, you seek *pleasure* by running away from those pains. You seek comfort in your favorite foods, alcohol, recreational drugs, cigarettes, gambling, etc. However, this pleasure is short lived and soon you are back to your usual state of sadness, unworthiness, jealousy, or guilt. Then, you run back to seek more pleasure. The more pain you have, the more you are going to seek pleasure. This obviously leads to *addiction*.

Running away from emotional pain and seeking momentary thrill, excitement, and pleasure is the basis of addiction.

The Monster Of Addiction

When the monster of addiction is acting out through you, you lose all control. Intellectually, you know that excessive food, cigarettes, alcohol, recreational drugs, etc. are damaging and you should not indulge in them, but you feel helpless in front of this monster. It's as if you have been enslaved by this beast. You feel *helpless*, which causes further emotional pain, which makes you want to escape more, and the vicious cycle of addiction continues.

Often, you try to keep your addiction to yourself and hide it from others. Why? Because there is a stigma of failure and bad behavior attached to it. Deep inside, you feel *ashamed* of yourself. So, you continue to suffer in isolation. You start to realize that no one really understands your pain. *Shame* and *Loneliness* get added to the heap of your emotional pain.

Harmful Effects Of Addictions On Health

Addictions wreak havoc on your physical, emotional, and spiritual health.

As we observed earlier in the book, *competition, comparison, judging, and guilt* trigger excessive release of adrenaline (and noradrenaline) and cortisol, which puts you at high risk of weight gain, Type 2 diabetes, infections, cancer, heart attack, high blood pressure, stroke, and dementia, to name a few.

True Freedom From Addictions

First, be honest with yourself and don't run away from your addiction. Instead, look deeper and only then can you see the mastermind of your addiction: your Acquired Self.

Then, you realize that you were *not* born with this addiction. No one is! It is not human nature.

You realize this addiction is the result of your Acquired Self, the Enemy within. With this realization, you can be free from the tight grip of your addiction.

Once you realize that the game of competition, comparison, judging, and the "book" of morality, ethics, traditions, and values are created by society, you start to see the true face of these concepts. You realize these concepts are part of the Acquired Self, but *not* the True Self.

Each time you have the urge to run for your escape to kill your sadness, jitteriness, emptiness, guilt, shame, loneliness, or boredom, realize that it is your Acquired Self luring you into these escapes. With this wisdom, rise above the urge to escape, and addiction will loosen its grip on you.

Each time you are free from your Acquired Self, you will find true peace and joy in your own True Self. The more you stay with your True Self, the less likely you will fall into the trap of addictions.

Alertness as well as awareness about the sneaky nature of your Acquired Self is extremely important. It is not *discipline,* but simple *awareness* about your Acquired Self that is the key to freedom from addictions.

CHAPTER: 36

OVEREATING AS AN ADDICTION

Overeating is the true pandemic of our time. It causes weight gain and obesity, with serious health consequences such as diabetes, high blood pressure, cancer, heart attack, stroke, gall stones, low back pain, etc.

Most people know these basic facts, but they continue to overeat. Over the years, I have *not* met a single obese person who does not understand the health hazards of obesity and who does *not* want to lose weight.

Weight Loss Techniques

Obese people want to lose weight, but most of them feel they can't do it alone. So, they seek out help. A lot of help is available in the form of weight loss programs, diet pills, dietary counseling, etc. However, this type of help works for the short term only. Most people gain back their weight once they are off the program. Obviously, they feel frustrated. They continue to jump from one weight loss technique to another. They go through the cycle of "weight loss and weight gain," and associated "happiness and sadness." Many give up for one reason or another. A lot of people get depressed.

What People Says About Their Struggle With Eating Habits

Being an endocrinologist, I frequently see patients with obesity. Here are some of the phrases I hear frequently:

- *"I have no discipline."*
- *"I am such a loser."*
- *"It's all my wife's fault."*
- *"I was doing so well until we went on the trip."*
- *"I will work on it, one day."*
- *"I need to lose 30 pounds for my daughter's upcoming wedding."*
- *"I can't control my eating when I go to parties."*
- *"I work so hard during the day. Then I reward myself in the evening by eating whatever I want."*
- *"I cheat here and there and that's enough to prevent me from losing weight, but I can't help it."*
- *"I know I stuff down my emotions, but I can't help it."*

- *"It seems like I do good for a while, but once I fall off the wagon, I can't get back on my strict regimen."*
- *"Sometimes I feel that I don't care. Then I eat food I know I shouldn't eat."*
- *"I eat excessively under social pressure, although I know better, but I can't help it."*

The Root Cause Of Overeating

To be free of overeating, you need to first get to the root of overeating behavior. Why does someone overeat? Look deeper and you'll see that overeating is due to learned habits of eating.

Where do you acquire habits of eating? From home, from school and from society in general, right?

Cultural Foods

First, you are downloaded with the concept of cultural foods as special food items. They keep a tight grip on us for the rest of your life. I remember a patient of mine once told me, "Doc, I can't stop eating pizza. I know it's bad for my health, but for God's sake, I'm an Italian. How can I ever stop eating pizza?"

Food Means Fun

All social occasions, including birthdays, weddings, religious, cultural, and national holidays are centered around food. That's how you acquire the concept of *"food means fun."* You can't imagine celebrating a certain holiday without the special food items that go with that holiday, no matter how harmful it may be for your health.

Food Equals Reward

You also learn that *food equals reward*. In schools, you are often promised ice cream or some other favorite food if you achieve certain points and grades.

Furthermore, you learn the concept that you are blessed if you have plenty of food. Remember your parents telling you, "How lucky you are to have such good food while there are so many hungry children in Africa."

Now what is opposite of reward? Punishment, right? So, when you discipline yourself *not* to eat your favorite food, it's as if you are punishing yourself. Therefore, over the weekend, you have the urge to reward yourself with plenty of your favorite food, no matter how unhealthy it may be. *That's how you get stuck in the cycle of punishment and reward.*

Emotional Eating

Often people eat to *stuff down their stress*. For example, all day, you work hard, dealing with stressful situations. Finally, you are at home, tired and exhausted from all the craziness that went on at work. You are ready to unwind, relax and enjoy. So, what do you do? You go for the food items that you love! "Come on, you deserve to have this **good** time after all the **bad** time you had at work," says your inner voice. This voice is so powerful that you completely ignore what your doctor told you or what you promised yourself last time you were on the scale.

People often stuff down their frustrations, sadness, loneliness, boredom, and guilt with food. Later, they feel even guiltier for breaking their diet… and the vicious cycle goes on.

Food As An Expression Of Love

Society also teaches you to express your love, friendship and gratefulness through food. These are all concepts, but you start to believe them to be important things.

Acquired Self Is The Basis Of Overeating

Perhaps now you understand that people overeat mostly for *psychological and social reasons* and not for *physiological reasons*. That's why we often eat when we are not even hungry, and we continue to eat even when we are no longer hungry.

All concept-based eating habits are part of your Acquired Self. While you identify with your Acquired Self, you obviously can't get rid of these habits and concepts. For example, how can you ever celebrate a birthday without cake?

As long as you are attached to the concept of birthday, you are going to have cake, even if you are diabetic or obese.

True Freedom From Overeating

Use common sense and realize that the root cause of your overeating lies inside you: your Acquired Self. Be free of your Acquired Self, and you will be free of your habits of overeating.

Remember the example I quoted earlier? (My patient who would not stop eating pizza because he was Italian.) I told him that he should tell himself that he is *not* Italian. The fact is that he *was not* Italian when he was born. He was *made* Italian by his parents. He could have been made French, Spanish, Indian, etc.

It is conditioning by our parents that makes us Italian, German, English, Christian, Muslim, Jewish, Hindu, etc. -all of which are concepts, right? These concepts become part of our Acquired Self. Then we start to believe them to be some kind of Truth.

To the Acquired Self, every concept is important because concepts are an important part of it. In reality, concepts are simply concepts and should be treated just like that. *Once my patient could see the conceptual nature of being Italian, he was able to be rid of this concept and with that, his lifelong attachment to pizza went away.*

Guidance To Be Free Of Overeating

- Realize, you are neither Italian, Mexican, Japanese, Armenian, Christian, Hindu, Buddhist, Muslim, Jewish, etc. You are a human being: no more, no less.
- All the so called "special days" are in fact concepts. In reality, there are *no* such things as birthdays, anniversaries, national holidays, religious holidays, etc. Even the Calendar is a concept created by the human mind.
- All emotional pain you carry comes from your past or imagined future, both of which are created by your mind. Certain events have happened but are not happening any longer except in your head. It is your mind that keeps them alive in the form of bundles of thoughts and emotions it calls "My past." In the same way, what the mind calls "My future" also consists of bundles of thoughts and emotions. See the true nature of the phantom of "My past and My future." With this logical insight, your emotional pains will simply melt away. Then obviously, there is no need to stuff down your emotions with food.
- You judge yourself and everyone else through the filters of "morality, values, traditions, etc." downloaded into your Acquired Self. You were not born with these concepts. Judging yourself and others creates a huge amount of emotional stress. That's why you have such a

hard time at work and even at home. Seeing the true nature of morality, ethics, values, and traditions will free you from the stress that arises out of *judging*.

- The book of "morality, values, and traditions" describes everyone's role. Naturally, it gives rise to expectations which are the basis of frustrations, annoyances, and anger, causing a hard time at work and at home.
- Goals, achievements, material possessions, status, success, and failure are all conceptual and in fact are the foundations for greed, ego, frustrations, jealousy, emptiness, loneliness, sadness, unworthiness, and bitterness. These emotions are the results of concepts created by the collective human mind and downloaded into your Acquired Self. Entertainment, excessive work, partying, and vacationing, are various escapes, and so is *excessive eating*. Look at the root cause of your emotional problems – your Acquired Self – and stop running to escapes.
- "Postponing" is another subtle, but very treacherous trait of the Acquired Self. By telling you to postpone, it keeps itself alive under the radar. However, there is no such thing as tomorrow. There is not even the next moment, but only this one! However, the Acquired Self fools you by creating tomorrow. You find yourself saying, "Oh, I understand I am overweight, but I will take care of it (tomorrow)." In reality, there is no "tomorrow." Yes,

you (or actually your Acquired Self) have a problem. Take care of it right *Now* by freeing yourself from the Acquired Self.

- Eat *only* to satisfy your hunger. "Food as Fun" is a concept deeply drilled into your Acquired Self by Society's Collective Acquired Self. Even "Fun" is a concept, an escape given to you by Society's Collective Acquired Self.

Pay Attention!

With this logical insight, you will be free of your Acquired Self. However, before you know it, it will hijack you again. *Paying attention is crucial.* Pay attention to the tempting thoughts or old eating patterns.

Practical Tips

- Be aware of temptations for certain food items that have become part of your Acquired Self such as ice-cream, chocolate, cake, candy, bread, desserts, etc.
- Pay attention when you are in the grocery store. Don't buy those food items you shouldn't eat.
- Pay attention to your food when you're eating. Taste every bite of it.
- Don't talk much during your meals because you can't pay full attention to eating if you're also having a conversation. For the same reason, don't surf the

internet, watch TV, or read newspapers while you're eating.

- Be at ease and take your time. Don't be rushed while eating your meal.
- Plan ahead for your next meal. Don't get trapped in the usual mind set of "Oh, it's too late to cook anything. Let's order pizza/fast food or find something to heat up in the microwave."
- Try to prepare your meals. Pay full attention when you're cooking.
- In general, eat only three times a day. Physiologically speaking, grownups don't need any snacks. Over the age of 50, most people only need two meals a day.
- Don't panic if you feel hungry in between meals if you are otherwise healthy, and you're not taking medications that can lower your blood sugar levels or you don't suffer from some medical disease that can cause low blood sugar. Physiologically speaking, you melt away the stored fat in your belly when you don't eat at the time of being hungry.
- Don't make "losing weight" some kind of mission or goal. This is what the Acquired Self loves to do. When you set up goals of any kind, you are in the grip of your Acquired Self, which will ultimately create stress for you. Stress causes excess release of a stress hormone,

cortisol, which causes more weight gain. How counterproductive your Acquired Self is!

- Simply live in the Now, be joyful, and stay free of the tight grip of your Acquired Self.

CHAPTER: 37

A WORLD OF CONCEPTUAL SEXUALITY

In the Human World, there is a concept about sexuality, which varies (somewhat) from society to society. However, the basic features are the same.

Basically, Society's Collective Acquired Self wants to control the sexual behavior of everyone living in it. Therefore, it has written rules about sexuality: when, where, with whom, and under what circumstances two human beings can engage in sexual activity. Any sexual activity outside of these rules is considered immoral/illegal/sinful, and may be punishable, which can be harsh in some cultures.

Sexuality In Nature

In contrast, sexual acts in nature between humans are meant for love and pleasure. It is a union between two souls.

When an animal reaches puberty, he/she seeks a willing partner and carries out the act of sex in nature, without any fear, shame, embarrassment, or any permission from an authority.

The sexual act in nature between consenting human adults is without any permission from some authority such as a marriage certificate.

Consequences Of Conceptual Sexuality

In the Human World, the concept of sexuality gives rise to several social, financial, and emotional problems such as:

- Fear of being caught, which often leads to anxiety, trauma, low self-esteem, premature ejaculation (in men), and frigidity (in women).
- Infidelity, which leads to emotional meltdowns, arguments, revengeful acts, divorces, etc.
- Pornography, which often leads to unnatural desires, unrealistic expectations, disappointments, worthlessness, anxiety, and depression.
- Prostitution, as a by-product of restrictions on sexual activity.
- Rape, because of various factors in the Acquired Self (psychological, social, developmental, and situational) that make a sexual act an act of ego, power, and control.
- Child molestation results from a variety of psychological, social, developmental, and

situational factors that are present only in the Human World.

In summary, sexual acts in the Human World are controlled by Society's Collective Acquired Self, which often leads to a variety of serious emotional, mental, and physical issues that do not exist in nature.

Freedom From Conceptual Sexuality

Once we realize how Society's Collective Acquired Self has made the *natural* act of sex so complicated and full of issues, we can be free of it. ***However, we still abide by the rules of society about sexuality.***

Above all, we realize that sex is a spiritual, wholesome act, and not an act of ego, power, control, possession, competition, or comparison.

We realize that a piece of paper (or mutual agreement) does not mean that the other person is now our sex slave.

We fully understand that sex is an act between consenting adults, no exceptions. Hence, there is no room for rape or child molestation. Sex is not only a physical union, but a union of two souls that makes us whole (one).

CHAPTER: 38

A WORLD OF ADHD – ATTENTION DEFICIT/ HYPERACTIVITY DISORDER

Attention Deficit / Hyperactivity Disorder (ADHD) is a relatively new medical condition. Unfortunately, an increasing number of children (as well as adults) are being diagnosed with ADHD. Often children are put on some drugs, so they are not disruptive in school. Unfortunately, these drugs have horrible side-effects. As a result, parents seriously struggle with the choice they must make for their children. Often, they succumb to tremendous pressure from schools and put their children on these dangerous drugs.

Is it possible to be free of ADHD without taking any drugs? Before you can answer this question, you need to look deeper at the root cause of ADHD.

What Is the Root Cause Of Attention Deficit / Hyperactivity Disorder?

The name, Attention Deficit /Hyperactivity Disorder basically describes the root cause of this disorder: There are two components of ADHD:

1. Attention deficit, lack of focus.
2. Hyperactivity, which takes the form of restlessness, impulsiveness, and disruptive behavior.

Why Doesn't Someone Pay Attention?

Because they have a busy mind. Now, what is a busy mind? It's your Acquired Self, isn't it? Hence, the root cause of attention-deficit is your own Acquired Self.

What Causes Restlessness?

A stream of excitatory thoughts triggers a chronic state of excitation and restlessness. As we observed earlier, thoughts come from the Acquired Self. Therefore, it is logical to conclude that the root cause of restlessness is also your own Acquired Self.

Development of ADHD

As we observed earlier in the book, the busy mind is a product of the downloading of concepts and information by society, which unfortunately, starts in early childhood.

Not too long ago, this downloading used to be in the form of books. Then came talking toys, movies, and video games. More recently, parents often give smart phones to their children (even when they are toddlers) to keep them engaged. In this way, parents don't have to be bothered to play with their children.

Furthermore, parents are instructed by Society's Collective Acquired Self to provide their children with as much mental stimulation as possible, so they are not intellectually left behind in school. This *mental stimulation* gets into high gear as they enter school.

It is amazing to see the type of information and concepts thrown at the brains of little children. Often, they learn the concepts of competition, comparison, judging, reward, punishment, victory, defeat, good, evil, fighting, wars, death, etc. Usually, this learning takes place through intense audiovisual stimulation with lifelike, graphic, sensational pictures and movies.

Overloaded with all kinds of stories, images, ideas, concepts, and information, a child's mind gets scattered. It runs in different directions like a wild horse. That is how lack of focus develops.

Arising out of incessant, uncontrollable thoughts, children also become impulsive, reckless, and at times destructive. They are easily distracted. Often, they stay in their own virtual world created by the busy mind, which often leads to learning difficulties in school.

Behavioral problems and learning difficulties in classrooms get the attention of teachers. Typically, parents are advised to take their children to a pediatrician, who comes up with the diagnosis of ADHD and prescribes drugs to control the symptoms.

Unfortunately, the root cause – the Acquired Self – conveniently escapes detection. That's how many individuals continue to suffer from some form of ADHD throughout their life.

True Freedom From Attention Deficit /Hyperactivity Disorder

Once, you – as a parent – realize that Acquired Self is the root cause of ADHD, you can help your child tremendously.

As all parents know, children follow what we do and *not* necessarily what we say. Therefore, you should free yourself from the tight grip of your own Acquired Self first.

Practical Tips For Parents

- Let children be children. Childhood is a time for joy, play, love, and curiosity.
- Try to keep your children away from the concepts of competition, comparison, and judging as much as you can. Be the example yourself.
- Spend time with your children instead of sending them off to a smart phone or video game. It will save you (and your children) a lot of headaches and suffering.
- Get your children involved with nature, such as spending time exploring nature, animals, plants.
- Guide them to develop manual skills.
- Teach them how to relax.
- Engage in stretching exercises, hiking, or jogging
- Guide them to find some manual hobbies where they must concentrate while having fun such as playing a musical instrument, painting, photography, gymnastics, dancing, swimming etc.
- Make sure to keep them away from competition, comparison and expectations.
- Love them unconditionally through your actions, and *not* just through lip service.

- Be the example that your children can follow and be free of stress.

CHAPTER: 39

A WORLD OF ESCAPES

In the Human World, most people suffer from tremendous emotional stress. If we use common sense, we can clearly see the mastermind of stress lies within us, the Acquired Self. Once we can see it clearly, we can be free of it. Then, we can get in touch with our True Self, the natural source of incredible joy, peace, and pleasure.

But Society's Collective Acquired Self does not allow us to be free of its tight grip. It does so by distracting our attention to the so-called "solutions for stress," which are basically **escapes** from stress. In this way, the Acquired Self stays under the radar and skillfully avoids detection. As a result, we stay trapped in the domain of Society's Collective Acquired Self. Here are a few examples:

Entertainment

Entertainment is a big part of the "Human World." It provides some temporary relief from emotional stress. That's why there is such a high demand for entertainment. It's no surprise that the lucrative industry of entertainment continues to explode, especially with the help of the Internet.

Vacations

When we get overwhelmed by the stress of daily living, we go on vacation, which may bring some temporary relief. However, travelling often adds to our overall stress as we deal with airport traffic, delays, cancellation of flights, rules and regulations, and expense of the travel itself. Not to mention travel illnesses, discomfort, disappointments, and frustrations.

Alcohol

Alcohol is a common escape in many parts of the world. By numbing the brain, it provides some temporary relief from stress. However, alcohol is a known toxin for the brain, nerves, liver, pancreas, and reproductive organs.

In addition, alcohol is a leading cause of addiction, roadside accidents, and violent behavior.

Alcohol often intoxicates relationships, and leads to emotional, mental, financial, and social problems.

Recreational Drugs

There is a long list of recreational drugs that are available in different parts of the world, each with its harmful effects on the body.

Additionally, these drugs are addictive, create havoc for relationships, and often result in emotional, mental, financial, and social problems.

Special Days

Society's Collective Acquired Self has also created so-called "Special Days," such as Birthdays, Anniversaries, New Year Day, Christmas, Thanksgiving Day, Eid, Diwali, etc. Then, there are independence days in most countries around the world.

Each of these "Special Days" are basically an excuse to have a party. On some "Special days," people get time off from work, which is nice.

Every "Special Day" has a certain protocol which itself creates plenty of stress. Often, people must travel long distances, spend a lot of money, be on time, behave in a certain way, and eat certain foods which are mostly unhealthy foods. In many countries, people also drink a lot of alcohol on these occasions. All these activities create a lot of physical, emotional and financial stress.

The social aspect of "Special Days" brings some happiness for a while. However, often people also get into competition, comparison, and even arguments, all of which create stress.

Hope

When stress created by the Acquired Self becomes unbearable and there is a chance we may discover the true face of the Acquired Self, it lures us into the fantasy land of tomorrow in the name of "hope." In this way, hope is an ultimate escape that almost everyone is trapped in.

Freedom From Escapes

Freedom from the mastermind of all stress – the Acquired Self – will liberate you from the lure of various escapes.

Once freed from the grip of the Acquired Self, you get in touch with your True Self, the source of eternal peace, joy, and love.

CHAPTER: 40

A WORLD OF TECHNOLOGY

Technology is a fundamental engine that has been driving the Human World since the dawn of civilization. It has continued to evolve with the evolution of the Human Conditioned Mind and Society's Collective Acquired Self.

Looking through filters of the conditioned mind, technology sounds marvelous. After all, it has helped humans become the dominant species on Planet Earth. Now, it's helping humans to explore other planets.

Society's Collective Acquired Self is so intoxicated with the marvels of technology that it is often *intolerant* to any criticism.

Let's sit on a neutral ground, free of the conditioned mind and observe the consequences of technology.

Note: I am sharing my observations. You may agree or disagree. That's all okay. Please be aware that I am not on any mission to change the world or turn people against technology.

The Basis Of Technology

Basically, the Acquired Self is *not* satisfied with nature. That's why it wants to *control* nature according to its wishes by developing technologies. Why? Because it is fearful of nature and wants to conquer it.

Technology Creates Problem When There Is No Problem

The Acquired Self sees a lot of problems in nature and creates technologies to fix the problems. Inadvertently, technology ends up creating problems that did not exist before. So, the Acquired Self comes up with more technologies to solve the new problem and the vicious cycle continues.

Along the way, the Acquired Self learned that technology brings in a lot of *money* and *power*. Hence, the greedy nature of the Acquired Self has become the driving force behind developing new technologies.

For example, the Acquired Self was not satisfied with the slow speed of walking. So, it came up with ever-evolving technologies (trains, motor vehicles, airplanes) that would drastically accelerate speed. Unfortunately, these technologies also *cut down* on walking. Mankind became sedentary, which created new problems: Obesity, diabetes, heart disease, stroke, dementia, cancer, lower back pain, sciatica, etc.

Instead of looking at the root cause of these newly created medical problems, the Acquired Self saw *opportunities* to make lots of money. So, it came up with drugs to control obesity, diabetes, heart disease, stroke, dementia, cancer, lower back pain, sciatica etc.

Drugs create new problems such as side effects, which the Acquired Self sees as opportunities to make more money. Hence, the Acquired Self came up with new technologies to deal with side-effects.

Locomotive devices also cause serious accidents, which create disabilities for those who survive the accidents. The Acquired Self makes new technologies to help disabled people and makes a lot of money along the way.

Locomotive devices also create huge amounts of stress from driving, stress to be on time, and avoid accidents, to name a few. Stress causes insomnia. headaches, anxiety, increase in blood pressure, diabetes, autoimmune diseases, etc. Hence, it creates drugs to manage these diseases. Drugs give rise to side-effects, which the Acquired Self see as more opportunities to make money. The money-making cycle continues.

In this way, the Acquired Self creates a never-ending series of problems, starting from something that was not a problem at all. ***Walking was obviously not a problem!***

Dysfunctional Aspect Of Technology

Technology itself is neutral. It is the Acquired Self which uses the technology that can make it good or bad. With few exceptions, technology is used for the interests of the Acquired Self such as power, money, greed, ego, hate, revenge etc.

Race For Power And Money

Some of the earlier technologies helped humans get an edge over their predators, survive hardships of weather, and grow their own foods.

But it was *not* enough. The Acquired Self developed a thirst for "power and money," a *thirst that cannot be quenched.*

The Acquired Self wanted to control land, seas, space, weather, other species. It simply wanted to *control* everything on the planet according to its wishes and make tons of *money* along the way.

For example, technology made it possible for humans to build basic houses for shelter - but that was not enough. Houses gradually become more complex: a place of water, electricity and fire, a storehouse of various types of machines, food items, arts and crafts, deluxe furniture and more lately, a place with internet, entertainment, climate control, etc. Imagine the amount of money being made by technology companies.

At the same time, modern houses create a host of health issues: Muscle and nerve diseases due to prolonged sitting, back problems from overly comfortable beds, cancer risk due to microwave ovens, just to name a few.

The Acquired Self also developed technologies to build trains, motor vehicles, roads and bridges to ride all over the land. In addition, it built ships to navigate the seas - but this was not enough. So, it also built airplanes to soar through the skies. Still not satisfied. So, it built rockets to go into space.

All these technologies generate incredible amounts of money. However, these technologies also create massive problems such as accidents, atmospheric pollution, climate changes, etc. Now, there are thousands of human-made objects in space cluttering the orbit and threatening to cause catastrophic events for Planet Earth.

Technology Of Warfare

Initially, technology helped humans gain power over their predators. However, it gradually became a vehicle to control fellow human beings. Spears, arrows, knives, swords, guns, tanks, fighter jets, bombs, missiles, and nuclear weapons are just some examples.

The evolution of technology has helped humans produce progressively deadlier weapons and there is no end to it. ***The train has left the station.***

In fact, technology – right from day one – got humans out of sync with nature. The underlying fear, (which was initially due to predators) grew exponentially and made humans extremely fearful of each other. ***Man became man's worst enemy***.

With the help of advancing warfare, they brought unthinkable suffering to each other.

Over Population

Thanks to our technology, we are no longer prey to our natural predators. Moreover, medical technology has helped us live longer. In addition, agricultural technology provides us with abundant food. Overpopulation is the natural consequence.

A Polluted World

Planet Earth has become a very polluted place, thanks to technologies such as motor vehicles, manufacturing industries, airplanes, oil drilling, plastics and much more. As a result, most humans breathe unclean air, drink polluted water and eat unhealthy foods.

A Pandemic Of Diseases

We are suffering from a pandemic of chronic diseases thanks to our modern lifestyle, which is a direct product of advances in technology.

Technology has made most humans sedentary. In addition, they consume too much food, because there is such an abundance of food. The food and agricultural industries use technological advances (preservatives, pesticides, weed killers, GMO foods, etc.) to alter foods so they can make more money.

The net result: a pandemic of obesity and chronic inflammation. Combine it with immense emotional stress, polluted air, polluted water, and living indoors (most of the time). This is a perfect storm for the pandemic of chronic diseases all around the world, which is getting worse every day.

A World Of The Internet

Computers and the Internet are relatively new technologies. However, these technologies have rapidly engulfed the entire human race.

Here are some consequences of the internet:

- An exponential expansion of the Virtual human world. Consequently, humans spend most of their time in the Virtual world and hardly any time in the Real world.
- A significant rise in medical disorders such as eye irritation and dryness, headaches, insomnia, anxiety, depression, paranoid behavior,

addictions, obesity, attention deficit, and daytime somnolence.

- Addiction: Most people are addicted to the internet. A smart phone has become a new “part” for the human body. People start having “withdrawal symptoms” if they lose their smart phone.
- Video games are especially addictive, causing isolation, paranoia, insomnia, aggressive behaviors, and breakdown of relationships.
- Social isolation – due to lack of actual human interactions – leads to depression, emotional eating, obesity, fear, and paranoia.
- Social media, news, information, entertainment, pornography, etc., have skyrocketed with good and bad consequences, depending on who is using this technology. For example, people can get *different* opinions about some incidence (event) in the world, from various political, religious, and cultural groups. People can seek alternatives to modern western medicine, which was almost impossible before the internet. People can get unbiased sex education, which was so rare before the internet. Authors and musicians can publish their work and reach thousands if not millions of people. In other words, the internet has brought

down the walls of "the establishment" created by political, religious, business, and cultural powers. However, there is also a massive increase in emotional stress: Thrills, excitement, sadness, fear, anger, grievances, bitterness, revenge, jealousy, paranoia, etc.

Arrival Of AI (Artificial Intelligence)

Despite all these issues – and warnings from the experts – greedy Acquired Selves continue to seek advancement in this technology, which has ushered in the era of AI (Artificial Intelligence). Its consequences are yet to be seen.

Like any other technology, its users will make it good and bad in the Human World. Most likely people will get even more consumed by the Virtual World than they are now.

A Word Of Wisdom

Some people (especially older folks who have seen life before and after the internet) complain about the issues that the internet has created. In this mindset of negativity, they generate more emotional stress for themselves. The fact is that Society's Collective Acquired Self has been in love with technology since the dawn of civilization. **There is no stopping technology.**

You should see technology for what it is: a tool to function in the human world. Don't develop any attachment to it, positive or negative. Use it when necessary and put it to rest when not needed. It is our ultimate choice! This is how we can be stress-free in this stressed-out world.

Section 3

Human Relationships

CHAPTER: 41

DRAMA AT HOME

All human interactions (with few exceptions) are basically interactions between Acquired Selves. As most Acquired Selves are charged with emotions, the interactions are also charged with emotions. Thus, there is emotional drama everywhere in "The Human World." Home is no exception. In fact, emotional drama is usually more intense at home than any other place.

Each Acquired Self primarily serves its own interests. It seeks to influence and control the behavior of others because deep down it is insecure. Basically, it harbors fear, anger, jealousy, and other emotions such as guilt, self-pity, sadness, and grief. Additionally, most Acquired Selves are competitive, greedy, and egocentric. Almost everyone judges and criticizes others. Many also suffer from self-criticism.

Love Changes Into Hate

Individuals typically fall in romantic love due to some shared concepts in their Acquired Selves, in addition to physical attraction and sexual desire. We can call it "Conditional Romantic Love."

Over time, Conditional Romantic Love between two Acquired Selves begins to fade, exposing the underlying layers of fears, insecurities, frustrations, expectations, and anger. Then, each Acquired Self attempts to mold the other according to their own wishes. This struggle for control almost always leads to heated arguments. Gradually, a sweet home turns into a battlefield where skirmishes become routine. Over time, the initial spark of love changes into the fire of anger and hate.

Sometimes, heated arguments may escalate into verbal and/or physical violence resulting in separations, divorces and legal disputes, leaving behind a trail of bitterness, anger, hate, and sometimes guilt and depression.

Freedom From Drama Of Romantic Love

"True love" remains an elusive ideal in "The Human World." Why? Because "True love" is present only in the absence of the Acquired Self.

True love requires individuals to be free of the prison of their own Acquired Self. Only then, can they see each other as human beings, not as a possession - "My girlfriend," "My wife," "My boyfriend," or "My husband."

In fact, it only requires one person to get enlightened for the relationship to become free of emotional drama.

Remember, it takes two hands to clap. One hand cannot clap. Therefore, instead of asking the other person to change, all you have to do is to rise above your own Acquired Self. You will be surprised to see how the entire dynamic of your relationship will change. The ripple effect of "True love" is magical. It has the power to liberate the other person from their Acquired Self. This type of transformation is from within, which is completely different from the battle of two Acquired Selves trying to control and subdue the other.

Once freed of the grip of the Acquired Self, you are in True love that never changes into hate. Then, home becomes heaven on earth.

Emotional Drama Around Children

In the Human World, parents fall in love with their children when they are little. However, soon parents start to download the contents of their own Acquired Self into their children, usually following what was done to them by their parents.

Parents often instill fear and paranoia in their children, saying things like "don't talk to strangers." They also introduce the concepts of competition, comparison, and judging, which cause a lot of stress for children. Inadvertently, parents create lots of stress for themselves as well.

As children become teenagers, emotional dramas at home and school start to escalate. Adolescents usually learn disrespect, rebelliousness, and adventurous (sometimes reckless) behavior from Society's Collective Acquired Self under the pretense that they are free birds.

Teenagers also experience peer pressure to fit in. Consequently, they often end up engaging in reckless behaviors such as alcohol, drugs, excessive partying, and indiscriminate sex.

Addiction to drugs, financial hardships, poor grades, and unwanted pregnancies simply add to the emotional issues of teenagers as well as parents.

Society's Collective Acquired Self tells parents and teachers to control their teenagers' behavior. In this way, Society's Collective Acquired Self skillfully turns parents, teachers, and teenagers against each other. Net result: a lot of emotional drama at home and school.

Freedom From Stress

For Teenagers, Parents And Teachers

If parents, teachers and teenagers could only clearly see the mastermind – Society's Collective Acquired Self, they could be free of its grip.

Once freed of the Acquired Self, our thoughts and actions are free of the emotions of fear, anger, bitterness, disappointments, worthlessness, and jealousy. We realize there is no need to prove anything. That's how teenagers can be free of peer pressure. Automatically, then they don't indulge in reckless behaviors such as excessive partying, indiscriminate sex, and drugs.

Once freed of the Acquired Self, parents and teachers no longer feel compelled to control their teenagers' behavior. Then, home and school become the true cradle of nurturing for children.

For more details, please refer to my book,

"Stress Management For

Teenagers, Parents And Teachers"

CHAPTER: 42

DRAMA IN EDUCATIONAL INSTITUTIONS

The Acquired Self's dominance is evident not only at home, but also in various systems of society.

Education systems, for instance, reflect the grip of the Acquired Self, emphasizing competition over cooperation and rewarding conformity rather than creativity. Students are conditioned to view their peers as rivals, striving for grades, awards, and prizes that symbolize societal praise and validation.

This conditioning continues into adulthood, where the pursuit of status and wealth becomes a measure of success dictated by Society's Collective Acquired Self.

Media and entertainment further reinforce the concepts of competition, comparison, judging, ego, and validation.

Social platforms also amplify this behavior, where likes and followers dictate self-worth.

On campuses, teachers, administrators, and students are simply a triangle of money, control and power, creating a ton of stress for everyone involved and beyond.

Freedom From Stress At Schools

Schools can become a true cradle of learning only if there is a stress-free environment, as our brains function a whole lot better when they are not under stress.

We can make schools stress-free only if we – professors, administrators, and students – are free of competition, comparison, ego, and judging.

CHAPTER: 43

DRAMA AT WORKPLACES

At workplaces, the Acquired Self manifests as competition, jealousy, and a relentless pursuit of money and power. It drives the need for validation, ego-enhancement, and greed, fostering environments where collaboration gives way to rivalry.

Workplace dynamics often prioritize productivity over well-being, creating cultures where individuals are pitted against each other in a relentless scramble for promotions, rewards, and recognition.

Most people don't perform well under stress. Consequently, productivity goes down, which puts more pressure on everyone in the organization. A vicious cycle that never ends.

Many people sacrifice personal aspirations and mental health for the illusion of professional success.

Bureaucratic hierarchies and rigid job descriptions further entrench this system, discouraging collaboration and innovation in favor of conformity.

Teamwork, though celebrated in theory, is often undermined by unspoken rivalries and the pressure to outperform one's peers.

Most workers are under intense pressure to meet deadlines. Others must deal with angry customers. They're trained that "the customer is always right." Hence, they must suppress their own anger for fear of losing their job. Some have the terrible job of laying off other employees to keep the company profitable.

Leaders are equally stressed out too, if not more. Most are under pressure to make their organization/company more successful and profitable, which makes them highly competitive and greedy, not only at work, but also in their social circle and even at home.

This culture of competition perpetuates a vicious cycle. The fear of failure and the lure of external validation ensure that the Acquired Self remains firmly entrenched, dictating not only how individuals perceive success, but also how they interact with colleagues, subordinates, superiors, and the organization at large.

Consequently, workplaces often become arenas of silent emotional drama, veiled behind polite exchanges and professional facades.

Fear of losing your job is on everyone's mind, no matter if you're a worker bee, head of a department, or CEO of a company.

Working in a stressful environment makes everyone stressed out, which wreaks havoc on emotional, physical, and spiritual health. That's why burnouts have become so common.

People often stay in the stressed-out environment of their job, because they don't see any alternative. In many cases however, they continue to work in a stressful environment, because it pays for their expensive lifestyle.

Some people leave one stressful job for another and are often disillusioned because they carry their own ambitions, greed, jealousy, self-righteousness, and ego with them. Ironically, they see these personality issues in everyone else except themselves. In the grip of the Acquired Self, they find every workplace full of stress.

Root Cause Of Stress At Workplaces

The virus of ego, competition, comparison, greed, self-righteousness, jealousy, and an insane pursuit of power and wealth plagues most workplaces. These are various components of the Acquired Self. Therefore, it is reasonable to conclude that the Acquired Self is the root cause of stress at workplaces.

How To Keep Workplace Stress Free And Joyful

Freedom from the Acquired Self automatically creates stress-free, peaceful, and joyful workplaces.

Freedom from the Acquired Self means freedom from the cage of ego, competition, comparison, greed, self-righteousness, jealousy, and insane pursuit of power and wealth.

Practical Tips:

- First treat everyone as a human being. Later, treat them as colleagues, employees, or bosses, etc.
- Socialize with an open heart. No one is your friend or enemy.
- Utilize your skills to do the job. Stay free of the ego that comes with titles like: CEO, president, CFO, director, administrator, chief, coordinator, organizer, collaborator, guest of honor, distinguished speaker, etc.
- Stay free of neediness for praise, validation, and recognition.
- Don’t ask for favors. Don’t provide any favors.
- Respect everyone sincerely, not just to their face.

- No one should be insulted, harassed, or embarrassed.
- Do not mix your love-life and professional life.
- Work cohesively for the overall well-being of the company, organization, agency, etc.
- The employer should provide well-being for its employees.
- Communicate freely and respectfully to clear any misunderstandings, instead of gossiping behind others' backs.
- Keep full attention at your work, without any interference from emotions.
- Now Breaks: Take short breaks (5 minutes) periodically to get in touch with the NOW: What you see, hear, smell, taste, and touch. Feel the glow of love in your chest.
- Work to simply make a living and *not* to be wealthy, powerful, or special.
- Keep your lifestyle simple, without any showoffs, unnecessary celebrations, and ego-enhancing objects and activities.
- Don't let your mind keep working all the time.
- Cultivate some non-mental, non-financial, non-egoic hobbies to feed your soul.

Section 4

Stress Free Living

CHAPTER: 44

FREEDOM FROM THE STRESSED-OUT WORLD

As we have observed in detail, the Human World is created by Society's Collective Acquired Self. It is conceptual, virtual, and full of political, social, cultural, financial, environmental, physical and emotional problems.

Your Acquired Self is a product of the Human World. It is constantly being fed by the Human World. Therefore, you must be free of the Human World, if you truly want to be free of your Acquired Self and live a stress-free, joyful, and peaceful life, free not only of emotional issues, but also medical and spiritual illnesses.

However, it does not mean you must renunciate the world or become a hermit. Quite the opposite. You live an active life full of joy, peace, pleasure, and unconditional love.

You can be free of the Human World by simply observing it, as we have already discussed.

Always use the light of common sense – innate intelligence (II) - that we are born with. Make sure *not* to develop any *negativity* towards your Acquired Self. Honor it but stay out of its tight grip.

Freedom From The Acquired Self

To live a stress-free life, you must be free of the tight grip of your Acquired Self. Then, you can utilize the Acquired Self as a tool to function in the Human World.

The Most Crucial Step:

Seeing your Acquired Self as a separate entity from yourself is the most important step to be free of its tight grip. A thorough understanding of the layers of the Acquired Self liberates you from its tight grip, as we have already discussed in this book. Only then do you see it as separate from you, simply a virtual entity, a useful tool to function in society!

Awakening

Once free of the prison of the Acquired Self, you automatically get in touch with your True Self and experience immense peace, joy, and unconditional love for everyone. This is called awakening or enlightenment. Once you get even a glimpse of this experience, you stay on this road. ***There is no going back.***

Awakening happens at different paces in different people. In some, it happens rapidly or even instantaneously, while in others, it is a slow process.

Practical Steps To Be Free Of The Acquired Self

1. Don't React Immediately

In the grip of the Acquired Self, we stay in auto mode. We react immediately to someone's comment or to our own inner voice.

Don't let your Acquired Self automatically take control of your thoughts, emotions, and actions. Pause before you react to someone's comment or action or even your own inner voice.

2. Shift Your Attention To The Now

Immediately, shift your attention to the Now – What you see, hear, smell, taste, and touch. Also, be aware of the space, silence, and stillness.

In addition, start counting your breath. After a little while, your emotional storm will calm down.

3. Use Logic

Now use logic, the most wonderful tool we humans have. Why? Because the Acquired Self is always illogical and can't stand the blazing sunshine of logic. Therefore, use logic and see the true colors of your Acquired Self. See for yourself who is really at the root of all your stress.

What is logic? When I use the word logic, I mean simple logic, the common sense that all we humans are born with. We don't need to go to school to learn it. Don't confuse it with "rationalization" that people often use to justify their actions. Rationalization, intellectualization, reasoning, and justification stem out of the Acquired Self.

To use your true, simple logic, you must be free from any conditioning. Otherwise, it will be tainted by your conditioned mind: all the concepts, opinions, ideas, beliefs, knowledge, and previous experiences swirling in your mind, which is your Acquired Self.

When you use simple logic, you clearly see your Acquired Self as the mastermind of all your stress.

The more you see your Acquired Self as a source of your stress, the more you become free of it.

See The Acquired Self In Action

Everyday living gives you the best opportunity to observe your Acquired Self. So, be aware of your Acquired Self in your everyday life. See it rising, trying to take control of you, and influencing your thoughts, emotions, and actions. Once you see it clearly and you know it's not your True Self, it starts to loosen its power over you.

That's how you get freedom from your Acquired Self. You don't fight it, hate it, or run away from it. Those actions will only strengthen it. Simply seeing it for what it is will liberate you from its tight grip.

EXAMPLES:

1. You are just about to point out to your wife one more time that she needs to lose weight. Stop for a moment. Use logic and you'll see that it's your Acquired Self at play: Your Acquired Self is fearful that she'll lose her health/looks and it wants to control her behavior.

Your wife's Acquired Self takes your advice as criticism, insult, or attack. In addition, her Acquired Self expected love, not criticism from her loving husband. So, her Acquired Self gets hurt and responds to your Acquired Self by defending itself: It puts up a wall of resistance and may fight back with an equally insulting remark.

Only when you fully realize the whole interaction is between two Acquired Selves, will you stop commenting about her weight. You'll be amazed how nicely she starts to respond to you.

2. When you are just about to complain to your husband that he's always glued to the TV (or smart phone) watching sports, take a pause and realize that it's your Acquired Self trying to control your husband's behavior.

3. When you are about to yell at your kid for not listening to you, pause and observe your Acquired Self. Once you clearly realize that it's your Acquired Self trying to control your kid's behavior, you will stop yelling at your kid.

Only then can you sit down and communicate with your kid with love and kindness. You will be amazed at the results.

4. Next time when you get upset or bored and start walking towards the refrigerator to pull out that carton of ice cream, stop for a moment.

Use logic and you'll clearly see that you are not hungry at all. So why eat it? Then, you will be able to see that it is your Acquired Self luring you and providing you with escape and sabotaging your health. Obviously, you can say "No" and get out of the habit of stress-eating.

5. Next time you see your anger rising because of your kids, parents, friends, employees, bosses, etc., pause for a moment and see clearly that it's your Acquired Self who is upset and outraged and wants to act through you. Only then can you say "No" to your Acquired Self and not act out in the way it wants you to.

Then, you can analyze the situation in a logical manner and take necessary steps to accomplish whatever needs to be done.

6. You are in your sixties and doing fine. Then one day, you read in the newspaper that someone important died of cancer. Your Acquired Self triggers a thought… What if I have cancer? This creates another thought of possibly losing your health, autonomy, and ultimately dying. This creates a huge amount of fear. You start feeling your heart pounding. You feel uneasiness and anxiety. Then you start wondering who'll take care of your wife if you die, which further worsens your fear and suddenly, you've got a full-fledged panic attack.

Even amid this panic attack, pause, take some deep breaths, and start counting your breaths. Look around and see what is happening in front of you. Feel the space inside your chest. Fully realize that it is your Acquired Self that is fearful. Your True Self – space, silence, stillness – is untouchable.

Then use logic. Ask yourself: Do I have cancer at this moment? Am I losing my autonomy at this moment? You realize that you really don't have any problems at this moment. Then, you clearly see that it is your Acquired Self playing tricks with you by creating an imaginary future.

The moment you clearly see the Acquired Self for what it is, an entity separate from you, it starts to loosen its power over you.

Using logic, you also tell your mind: "I will deal with any medical condition, if and when it arises." Stress completely evaporates and you move on with your everyday life.

7. If someone insults you, typically you immediately fight back by insulting that person. Often the other person fights back and then you fight back, too. Before you know it, this verbal fight may escalate into a physical fight.

Some people don't fight back verbally or physically at that moment, but they continue to harbor bitterness against that person and seek opportunities to take revenge. In either case, you create a lot of stress for yourself and the other person.

On the other hand, once you have already gained the wisdom of not reacting immediately to people's remarks, you can pause for a moment. Feel the anger rising inside you. You can also clearly see that it's not the True you, but your Acquired Self who is outraged. With a little more logic, you also see the one who is insulting you is doing so under the influence of his/her Acquired Self. Then, you don't hold any bitterness, grudge, or hate towards that person.

Once your Acquired Self has calmed down, you may say something or take some action which will be a whole lot more effective and will not create stress for yourself or the other person.

Don't Be Frustrated If You Are Unable To See Your Acquired Self

Sometimes, you may not be able to take a pause and before you know it, you have said or done something under the influence of your Acquired Self.

After a while, you realize what actually happened and are able to take a logical look at the whole incident…. And that's okay. It takes practice to change your life-long conditioned-patterns. However, as long as you can see these reactions as a function of your Acquired Self, you are getting freedom from your Acquired Self.

For example, someone cuts you off on the freeway. You feel enraged and as a knee jerk reflex, you honk or give them the finger. Once your rage settles down, if you can see with logic what really happened, you can be completely transformed.

Let's examine this whole drama with logic. It's your Acquired Self and the other driver's Acquired Self in full action, isn't it? His Acquired Self wants to win, get ahead, and is thrilled at victory. On the other hand, your Acquired Self feels like a loser and tries to fight back.

Once you can clearly see your Acquired Self, the next time you will relax and laugh at your own Acquired Self. Instead of fighting back, you'll continue to drive safely. Stress will not even touch you.

Stay Alert And Vigilant

Often, your Acquired Self will try to trick you back into your old habitual thinking and reactions. Therefore, it is important to stay alert and vigilant. Keep seeing your Acquired

Self in action with vigilant eyes. You may even be amused or break into laughter when you observe how ridiculous and persistent your Acquired Self is... how it wants you to believe in something that is not happening at all in the Now. The moment you can see your Acquired Self as an acquired virtual entity, but *not* who you really are, it starts to loosen its power over you. With this realization, you'll see the thoughts triggered by your Acquired Self fading away. Often, you will need to see your Acquired Self many times before you are finally free of it.

Do Not Underestimate The Power Of Your Acquired Self

Do not underestimate the power of your Acquired Self. It has strong roots and will do all it can to control your thoughts, emotions, and actions. After all, it consists of your life-long mental habits, ideas, traditions, and belief system, all of which were bestowed upon you by your loving parents and society. It also consists of your own experiences, which in addition to psychological pain, also holds sweet memories.

"How can I get rid of all of this?" says your Acquired Self and puts up a wall of emotional resistance. "After all, everyone else is like me so this must be my true nature." Your Acquired Self tries to convince you and may even succeed temporarily.

However, if you're determined and pay attention to the Acquired Self, you'll be amazed how it starts to loosen its power over you.

Various Components Of The Acquired Self

It is relatively easy to see the so-called negative components of the Acquired Self such as competition, comparison, judging, bad memories, what if syndrome, etc. - But it is much more difficult to see the so-called good components of the Acquired Self such as good memories, noble ideas, heroic missions, etc.

To be free of the Acquired Self, you need to see it all, in all its colors, shapes, and forms.

Transformation Automatically Takes Place

Once you realize that you are separate from your Acquired Self, a process of transformation begins. Your daily life gives you plenty of opportunity to see your Acquired Self in action. Each time you see it as an entity separate from the True you, it loses power over you. Then, instead of being upset with someone, you will be grateful that their so-called bad remarks or behavior provided you with the opportunity to see your own Acquired Self and be free of it.

In Summary

Utilize your Acquired Self to function in society. Also beware how it can easily steal your identity and start to create emotional thoughts and actions.

Take the following steps while interacting with others in your daily life:

1. Stay in the Now: What you see, hear, smell, taste, and touch. Also, be aware of space, silence, and stillness.
2. Realize you are not the Acquired Self. You are separate from the Acquired Self.
3. Pause and don't react immediately to people's comments or your own inner voice.
4. Instead, shift your attention to the Now.
5. See for yourself how your Acquired Self creates stress for you.
6. Stay aware and vigilant.
7. Don't get frustrated if you sometimes fail.
8. See the Acquired Self in all its colors, shapes and forms.

CHAPTER: 45

HOW TO LIVE A STRESS-FREE, PEACEFUL, AND JOYFUL LIFE

As we have observed in this book, we live in two worlds: the Real World, and the Human World.

The Real World was created by the Real Creator whereas the Human World was created by the Collective Human Mind. It is virtual and conceptual.

The Real World is free of any emotional stress, whereas the Human World is full of emotional stress.

We are born with our True Self that helps us to function in the Real World, but as we grow up in society, we acquire another self, the Acquired Self, that helps us to function in the Human World.

Unfortunately, the Acquired Self steals our identity. Then, all we see is the Acquired Self. Instead of being a tool to function in the Human World, it becomes us. Then, it controls our thoughts, emotions, and actions. In this way, it creates tons of emotional stress for us and everyone else around us. Collectively, it creates a very stressed-out Human World.

The secret to living a stress-free, peaceful and joyful life is to stay anchored in the Real World (and True Self), while functioning in the Human World, utilizing our non-emotional, functional component of the Acquired Self.

Practical Steps To Stress-Free, Peaceful, And Joyful Living

After my awakening, I became free of my Acquired Self as well as the Human World. It all happened in a moment. The wisdom simply sank deep in my fabric.

However, I did not leave the Human World. Instead, I chose to continue to live in it. That's why I understand the challenges of living in the Human World and how to live a stress-free, peaceful life, which is also filled with immense joy, pleasure, and love.

Here are practical steps that I recommend, based on my own experiences:

1. Wisdom

Have a thorough understanding of the Acquired Self, the True Self, the Human World, and the Real World, which we have discussed in detail in this book.

2. Live In The Now

Keep your attention in the NOW, as much as you can.

Realize the difference between the **Virtual Now** and the **Real Now**. The Virtual Now is in your head whereas the Real Now is in front of your eyes and inside you. It is the field of awareness created by your senses: what you see, hear, smell, taste, touch and otherwise perceive. Furthermore, pay attention to space that gives rise to objects, silence that gives rise to sounds, and stillness that gives rise to movements. This is the Real Now.

Space, silence, stillness is the canvas for the painting of the universe. What is the universe? Space (and all objects in it), silence (and all sounds in it), stillness (and all movements in it).

The more you stay in the Real Now, the more you become aware of it. At some point, you will realize space, silence, stillness are not three separate entities, but one – the Creator of all objects, sounds, and movements.

3. Simplify Your Life

Continue to live in the Human World but make some changes to simplify your life. Once you feel the simple joy of being, you don't *need* to take vacations, watch movies, or celebrate so-called special days. In addition, you don't *need* alcohol, cigarettes, or recreational drugs to feel happy or to numb your emotional pains.

Additionally, you will have no desire to gamble, spend a lot of money on powerful cars, or pay premium prices for entertainment.

Once you realize you don't have to impress other people to gain praise and validation, you will automatically stop buying/leasing expensive houses, cars, clothes, shoes, jewelry, etc... Imagine how much money you can save by simplifying your life.

Once you realize that you don't need to make a lot of money to meet your needs, you automatically get out of the rat race.

Once you are free of attachment to your career, you will be able to retire early once you have saved enough money to continue simple living.

Once your life is not consumed by excessive work, you will have time for joyful activities such as cooking, gardening, painting, photography, playing musical instruments, dancing, dating, hiking, biking, going to the gym, swimming, sitting in a steam room or sauna, etc.

4. Relationships

Once you are free of the grip of your Acquired Self and the Human World, you interact with everyone on a human basis first. Secondarily, they may be your spouse, children, friends, colleagues, bosses, employees. In this way, no one is automatically honorable, senior, superior, junior, or inferior. You enjoy their company wholeheartedly. You engage in meaningful conversations. You may also be lighthearted and joke around but without insulting anyone.

Once you are *not* in the total grip of "the book of role descriptions" you have no expectations. Hence, no disappointments, frustrations, or anger. You try to do your part right, but don't expect others to play by the book.

In addition, you don't judge any person. Hence, you are free of the concepts of good, bad, like, dislike, love, and hate.

You don't judge yourself for some tragic event that was out of your control. Therefore, you are free of self-criticism and guilt.

You are free of the game of competition and comparison. Hence, you are free of ego, thrills, excitement, humiliation, sadness, unfairness, and anger.

Once free of ego and self-righteousness, you can have meaningful conversations and dialogues without getting angry.

You are also free of the game of praise and insults. In addition, you are free of the grip of hypocrisy, prejudice, embarrassment, shame, rudeness, and politeness.

Once you are free of the tight grip of insecurity, you are not afraid of others' reactions. Hence, you are not afraid to speak out and express your opinion.

Once you are not in the total grip of morality, still you *try* to do things right, such as being honest and truthful. However, you are also practical and may resort to "white lies" if, for instance, you have to protect your personal information from fraudulent people. Free of fear, you don't easily provide your personal information to fraudulent people who may send you fake threatening orders and requests.

In addition, you don't strictly follow society's rules as long as bending the rule does not hurt you or someone else.

If you get in a stressful situation at home or at work, you are not afraid to leave it. However, you also accept it wholeheartedly if you cannot leave the situation.

You realize you don't own your spouse, children, parents, friends, etc. Hence, there is no need to control their behavior. However, you may point out your opinion.

The only exception is small children who need your guidance and supervision.

Free of possessiveness, you don't get jealous. In addition, you don't feel sad if a relationship breaks apart. You also don't go through immense grief when some friend or family member passes away.

5. Joyful Socialization

Socialize without any preconceived ideas or agenda. Meet other humans in public places such as streets, schools, shops, restaurants, parks, gyms, but always with an open mind and a big smile.

Most people – in the grip of their Acquired Self – try not to engage with strangers. They feel comfortable – and socialize – with their old friends or friends of friends. In this way, they usually have a limited group of friends. But once you are free of the Acquired Self, you love to meet new people every day. You have no fear of strangers. Also, you are not timid or afraid of rejection. Free of your Acquired Self, you don't try to convince, subdue, or convert the other person. You are also free of obsession to win arguments. Therefore, interactions are joyful. In this way, you keep enjoying the company of humans everywhere and all the time, not just at organized social events.

6. Joyful Solitude

Socialization is important, but so is solitude. Keep a balance in life. Spend some time alone, especially in the morning or before going to bed. Take a hot bath. It is more relaxing if you add Magnesium Sulfate (Epsom Salt), and light up some incense. It is a wonderful time to practice staying in the NOW: What you see, hear, smell, taste, and touch. Also, pay attention to space, silence, and stillness - the canvas for the painting of the universe.

Feel the warmth of the water all over your body. Do some stretches while in the bathtub.

After bathing, towel-dry your skin and gently massage all parts of your body, as if talking to each part and being grateful for their support. You may use some oil depending upon your skin type. For example, use sesame oil or Mahanarayan oil if you have thin, dry, cold skin, On the hand, if you have thick, warm skin, use coconut oil.

Afterwards, you can do stretches, go for a morning walk or go to sleep if it's bedtime.

7. Adequate Sleep

Get sufficient sleep, which is about 7 – 8 hours. Remember, our physical body rejuvenates during our sleep at night. In addition, our soul gets in touch with the Universe.

Please read more about soul in my book,

"Wake Up While You Can."

Unfortunately, most people don't get enough sleep due to a variety of reasons such as work, parties, late dinners, spending time on the internet, etc. Many suffer from insomnia.

What Causes Insomnia?

- Acquired Self in the form of a busy mind. It may be worried, excited, or angry.
- Caffeine
- Bright lights in the house.
- Bright screens of TV, computers, and smart phones
- Late night dinners and partying
- Jet lag due to long distance air travels

8. Nourish Your Body

Lately, eating has become enormously complicated in the Human World, thanks to so many new concepts added by so-called experts, political, cultural, and religious groups. Consequently, food has become food-industry, an opportunity for businesses to make a lot of money.

Being an internist and endocrinologist, I am well-versed with our body's metabolism and nutritional requirements. I am also well-aware of dietary concepts such as calories, macronutrients, Paleo diet, Protein power, Mediterranean diet, Vegetarian diet, Vegan diet, etc.

Since my awakening, I developed a common-sense approach to nutrition, put it into my medical practice and observed good results.

Here Is An outline of this approach:

- Always *listen* to your body. It will guide you, what and what not to eat. Also use common sense.
- In general, stick with the type of foods that your ancestors have been ingesting for thousands of years. Your body has inherited cumulative Innate Intelligence from their eating experiences. Therefore, it can digest *certain* foods better than others. In addition, it also *needs* certain foods that your ancestors have been eating for thousands of years. Therefore, stay vegetarian if your ancestors were vegetarians. Stay non-vegetarian, if they were non-vegetarians.
- Everyone's nutritional requirements are different. Therefore, one-size-fits-all approach is unscientific. For example, eat less if you are overweight and eat more if you are underweight.
- Try to eat fresh foods as much as possible. Why? Because the most important ingredient in our food is *life* energy which starts to decay over time. Therefore, do not eat leftovers. For the same reason, try to grow your own fruits and vegetables.
- What type of fruits and vegetables to eat? It depends upon the season. Different fruits and vegetables grow in different seasons. There is immense natural wisdom in it. Unfortunately, these days fruits and vegetables are transported all over the world. For example, in winter,

you may get produce that grows in summer in another region of the world. It may be good for businesses, but not for your health. Avoid fruits and vegetables grown under unnatural conditions such as hydroponics.

- Avoid any food that is commercially altered such as GMO fruits and vegetables, growth hormone fed poultry, and other meats that are also given antibiotics. Say *no* to candies, snacks, highly processed meats, etc. Look for produce that is grown *naturally* without pesticides and fertilizers.
- Not too long ago, everything grew organically (the term organic did not even exist). Now, you must pay extra to buy organic foods. That's okay! Don't develop any negativity. Simply observe how the Collective Human Mind has created technologies to alter foods in its pursuit of greed.

9.Sensible Exercise

Everyone's exercise needs are different. Therefore, one-size-fits-all recommendations are unscientific.

Most people are either sedentary or overzealous in their exercise routine. Be neither because both extremes are unhealthy. (Remember, extremes are always to be avoided).

Exercise according to your body's needs. You may exercise more if you are overweight or young, but your body will likely need less exercise if you are old and thin.

What type of exercise? Walking is the best exercise. You may also want to do stretches before and after walking. Also, walk followed by stretches throughout the day in short spurts.

10. Massages

Massages on a regular basis can be an important tool for your overall physical, emotional, and spiritual health.

Massage comes in many forms. Most massages provide deep relaxation and help to relieve physical and emotional stress of daily life. Lomi Lomi (traditional Hawaiian massage) is particularly good in this regard.

Other massages such as Deep Tissue, Myofascial release (MFR) and Acupressure can help to deal with illnesses due to emotional and physical stress such as chronic pain, headaches, and fibromyalgia, to name a few.

11. Sexual Health

Sexual health is an important part of stress-free joyful living.

We are naturally sexual beings. When we reach puberty, we have an intense desire to find a mate. However, the Human World tries to *control* this natural urge by creating concepts such as “sex is sinful,” or sex should be carried out under certain rules and conditions.

Instinct of sex and society's strict rules about sexuality create conflict, and stress, with serious emotional consequences as well as physical illnesses.

Many people try to conform to societal versions of sexuality while others rebel. Either way, it causes a lot of emotional issues. There is a middle-of-the-road approach.

Realize that societal versions of sexuality are simply a concept. Respect it, but don't get enslaved by it. Figure out a way to carry out your natural sexuality by bending societal rules as long as it does not harm you or someone else.

Tips About Healthy Sexuality:

The best time to have sex is in the morning. That's when your testosterone level is at its peak.

Please note that testosterone is not only present in males, but also in females and plays a vital role in their sexual libido.

If you are married or in a relationship, try not to sleep in the same room. You get used to your partner's body. In addition, you start to take it for granted, which often ruins your sexual libido.

When you don't take your partner for granted, there is a natural element of curiosity. Then, you engage in flirtation, trying to get your partner's attention.

Sexual acts should be enjoyable for both parties. In heterosexual relationships, it takes a while for women to warm up, while men are ready in a heartbeat and may be finished by the time a woman is ready. That can make sexual acts for women unsatisfactory and even painful. After repeated episodes of such unpleasurable acts, many women don't want to engage in sex, but they also don't want to lose their husband (or boyfriend). So, they engage in sexual acts half-heartedly. Often, their male partners wonder why there is no passion.

It all stems from a lack of open communication, which erodes sexual relationships, and can create emotional issues such as premature ejaculation, low self-esteem, and lack of confidence in men and frigidity in women. All these issues can be avoided with open communication.

Sex is more than a physical act. It is a union of two souls. Hence, it is a *spiritual experience*. If done right, you can feel this union. You both become ONE.

Spiritual Sex

The important spices to spiritual sex are total relaxation, slow pace, plenty of time, and no expectations. Stay in the Now, listen and respond to each other's body, while looking into each other's eyes, as eyes are windows to the soul.

12. Dietary Supplements

We are often low in vitamins and minerals, thanks to our modern lifestyle and commercial farming practices as well as storage, transportation, and distribution of food through mega grocery stores.

In addition to growing your own fruits and vegetables, consider taking the following supplements:

Daily Vitamins For Health

- Vitamin D3 with K2
- Magnesium
- Zinc Plus Copper
- Iodine
- Multivitamin

Herbs For Relaxation

Here is list of the best herbs for stress relief, backed by scientific studies.

- Ashwagandha
- Holy Basil
- Rhodiola
- Bacopa
- L. Theanine
- Lemon Balm
- Passion Flower

To learn more about these dietary supplements, please go to my website: ZIOHH.COM

13. Only Necessary Tests and Drugs

These days medical doctors often recommend many unnecessary tests and drugs, which not only cause financial issues, but may also cause harm to your physical health.

For example, some physician may recommend "Whole Body CT Scan." You may think highly of your doctor, that they are being thorough. The fact is your physician is not a good clinician and heavily relies on tests. Not a good doctor! In addition, Whole Body CT Scan exposes you to a high dose of radiation and increases your risk of cancer.

Many so-called preventive care tests are actually diagnostic tests. For example, a colonoscopy can diagnose cancer but will not *prevent* colon cancer. Similarly, mammograms can diagnose cancer but will not *prevent* breast cancer. It is your healthy lifestyle that may prevent cancer.

These days doctors also recommend unnecessary drugs. For example, cholesterol lowering drugs (such as STATIN drugs), stomach acid reducing drugs (Proton Pump Inhibitors such as Omeprazole,) and antibiotics are overprescribed. These drugs have significant side-effects.

Many physicians seem to have forgotten the Hippocratic Oath – First Do No Harm – which has been the foundation of medical ethics for ages.

Always ask your doctor, "What is the risk versus the benefit ratio," a golden rule that has been the standard of medical practice.

Unfortunately, many physicians have a limited knowledge about the side-effects of drugs as well as their interactions. Why? Because they have no time (as well as no interest) to dig deeper. Therefore, do your own homework and read for yourself. However, be careful which sites you go to, as there is a lot of misleading information out there.

Websites such as PubMed and Drugs.com are reliable sources.

Equipped with some good information, you can have a more productive conversation with your physician. Take charge of your health, because no one else can. Health care providers can only give you advice. Ultimately, it is your body, and you are responsible for taking care of it.

14. Making Decisions

In life, we are making choices all the time. Unfortunately, we often make decisions while we are upset or fearful. These emotion-laden decisions usually create stress.

Remember a simple rule of thumb: Whenever you are faced with some challenging situation, shift your attention to the Now, relax completely, and think with a clear head, not through your emotions of fear, anger, jealousy, etc. Simply ask the question and go on with your life.

Often, you will get an answer sometime later. You will know it is the right choice in your deepest layers of the soul.

15. Meditation Practice

Here is a *guide* you can follow. Parents can practice it themselves and then share it with their children in a way that suits their age.

- Sit quietly in a comfortable chair (or on the floor in crisscross if you can) and relax. No music, telephone, TV or any other distractions.
- Pay attention to your surroundings: what you see, hear, smell, taste, and touch.
- Pay attention to *space* in which everything is, *silence* which gives rise to all sounds, and *stillness* in which all events take place.
- Pay attention to your breathing. Observe how your chest expands with inhalation and retracts with exhalation. Count your breaths.
- See how thoughts are chasing each other. Treat them as thoughts and no more. They are thoughts, but not *you*. Whatever they imply is not happening.
- Keep your attention in the Now.
- Feel inner peace and joy.

CHAPTER 46

PURPOSE OF LIFE

We are all here for a purpose. Unfortunately, we forget about it as we get in the grip of the Acquired Self. Then, we *mistakenly* think the purpose of life is to be successful, make a lot of money, grab as much power as possible, seek a lot of praise and validation, have as much entertainment as possible, etc.

Here is the outline of true purpose of life and how to achieve it.

AT SPIRITUAL LEVEL

To experience REAL GOD inside you and around you. Unfortunately, no one – with few exceptions – experiences REAL GOD. Why? Because their attention is sucked up by the conditioned mind – The Acquired Self, which keeps them trapped in the conceptual human world. Then, you live your life through the concepts that the human mind has created – which has even created the concept of GOD.

Your soul starts out free of any concepts and emotions, but then it adds a load of emotional burden through each lifespan that it lived in the human world, full of concepts. Now, imagine the incredible number of lifespans your soul has already gone through. Imagine the tremendous amount of emotional burden it already accumulated even before it started its most recent journey through this lifespan. Unfortunately, it stays asleep and keeps adding more emotional burden every day.

This lifespan gives you a great opportunity to get rid of the piled up emotional burden of the past – and not to add any more emotional burden. So, when your physical body dies this time around, your soul will be liberated as a truly FREE SOUL, as it was at the beginning.

Rise above your Acquired Self with wisdom. In this way, you don't generate any more emotional burden. Live in the REAL NOW and experience REAL GOD.

At Physical Level

Try to reproduce and nurture your children until they are physically able to be independent. In this way, life perpetuates, because life lives in life forms only.

EXPERIENCING THE DIVINE

One day I was having lunch alone at a restaurant, keeping my attention in the Real Now, when I experienced the Real Creator. Afterwards, a floodgate of spirituality opened up, which I describe in a non-religious spirituality book,

"Wake Up While You Can."

FINAL THOUGHTS

If you have reached this page, pat yourself on your back for reading a book that can enlighten you and transform your life, but only if you put into practice what you have learned.

If you have any questions, feel free to contact me at info@doctorzaidi.com

With Warm Regards,

Sarfraz Zaidi, MD

ACKNOWLEDGEMENTS

I would like to express my gratitude towards my wife and soulmate, Georgie Zaidi, for her careful and detailed proofreading.

I am also thankful to random strangers who welcome my ice-breaking efforts and engage in somewhat deep conversations about life. Many have become acquaintances and friends.

In addition, I am so grateful to my former patients who gave me the opportunity to observe the impact of my stress cure approach on their health issues.

Other Books by Sarfraz Zaidi, MD

Wake Up While You Can

A New, Logical, Non-religious Insight Into Life After Death

Sarfraz Zaidi, MD

You Are Not
Who You Think You Are

Poems that can awaken you

Sarfraz Zaidi, MD

POWER
OF
VITAMIN D

A VITAMIN D BOOK THAT CONTAINS THE MOST SCIENTIFIC, USEFUL AND PRACTICAL INFORMATION ABOUT VITAMIN D - HORMONE D

Brand New Chapter on Vitamin D and COVID-19

Sarfraz Zaidi, MD

Reverse Your Type 2 Diabetes

Scientifically

Get The Facts

And

Take Charge Of

Your

Type 2 Diabetes

Sarfraz Zaidi, MD

Hypothyroidism
And
Hashimoto's Thyroiditis

A
Groundbreaking,
Scientific
And
Practical
Treatment
Approach

Sarfraz Zaidi, MD

GRAVES' DISEASE
AND
HYPERTHYROIDISM

What You
Must Know
Before
They Zap
Your Thyroid
With
Radioactive
Iodine

Sarfraz Zaidi, MD

All books are available at Amazon.com,

other online retailers

as well as libraries and traditional bookstores.

You can also access them from

Dr. Zaidi's Website

ZIOHH.com

Contact us: contact@doctorzaidi.com

www.ingramcontent.com/pod-product-compliance
Lightning Source LLC
LaVergne TN
LVHW010637110826
845149LV00014B/2861

* 9 7 8 0 9 8 8 7 8 4 4 7 5 *